Child Care and ABC's Too

CHILD CARE & ABC'S TOO

Sar A. Levitan
Karen Cleary Alderman

THE JOHNS HOPKINS
UNIVERSITY PRESS
Baltimore & London

This study was prepared under a grant from the Ford Foundation.

The Johns Hopkins University Press, Baltimore, Maryland 21218
The Johns Hopkins University Press Ltd., London

Library of Congress Catalog Card Number 75-11355
ISBN 0-8018-1733-1

Library of Congress Cataloging in Publication data will be found on the last printed page of
this book.

Sar Levitan is professor of economics and director of the Center for Manpower Policy Studies
at the George Washington University. Karen Cleary Alderman is a research associate with the
Center for Manpower Policy Studies. They collaborated in writing *Old Wars Remain Un-
finished: The Veteran Benefits System.*

Photographs in this book are reproduced courtesy of *Manpower Magazine* and the Office of
Child Development, Department of Health, Education, and Welfare.

CONTENTS

PREFACE

The steady growth in the number of mothers working outside the home has created a demand for child-care arrangements. Predictions that child care would develop into a major growth industry during the 1970s have not materialized, however. A 1971 presidential veto of a bill that would have expanded federal support, the expense of institutional child care, and the preference of many mothers for flexible home care have slowed the growth of formal child-care arrangements. Nonetheless, expenditures for the care and education of children under age six have continued to grow, and child care is now a $6 billion industry. Still, the demand for suitable child care remains frequently unfilled. Public school systems have shown an increasing interest in "preprimary" children as the declining birth rate has decreased the supply of six-year-olds. But the schools are not equipped to fill the needs of children whose mothers have full-time jobs. The search for new institutional arrangements, including the delivery of early compensatory education to poor children, is therefore continuing.

This volume reviews the current American child-care system. It focuses on the role of the federal government in the expansion of child care and emphasizes the needs of children from poor homes. A survey of the demographic and economic characteristics of working mothers (chapter 2) is followed by an analysis of the provisions these women make to care for their children and by estimates of the degree to which more readily available child care might affect the labor force participation of mothers. Chapter 4 is devoted to a discussion of child-care costs and attempts to determine who picks up the growing tab for the care and education of children under six years old. The subsequent chapter traces the development of nursery and kindergarten education in the United States and examines the reasons for the educational system's interest in expanding school attendance to include children below the traditional age of five or six. The chapter also assesses how much education might profitably be dispensed to young children before they reach the traditional school age. Chapters 6 and 7, devoted to the federal role in expanding child care, survey the special services available to poor children and examine the role of the federal government in funding compensatory education to children from low-income families. The final chapter indulges in crystal-ball-gazing about the future of child care in the United States.

The volume has benefited from the critical comments and counsel of child-care experts. Officials of the Department of Health, Education, and Welfare and of the Department of Labor have been generous with their help in the preparation of this study. We are indebted to William Diepenbrock and William R. Prosser, Department of Health, Education, and Welfare, and Pearl G. Spindler, Department of Labor. Gilbert R. Austin, University of Maryland, and Dana Hay, The George Washington University, also shared their perspectives and contributed critical comments on the manuscript. Robert Taggart, National Manpower Policy Task Force, and William Johnston, Center for Manpower Policy Studies, The George Washington University, contributed organizational and editorial assistance.

This volume was prepared under a grant from The Ford Foundation to the George Washington University's Center for Manpower Policy Studies. In accordance with the Foundation's practice, complete responsibility for the preparation of this book was left to the authors.

Sar A. Levitan
Mother's Day, 1975   *Karen Cleary Alderman*

Child Care and ABC's Too

CHAPTER ONE / THE AMERICAN
CHILD-CARE SYSTEM

       Much has been written about the care of children under six years old and about whether the United States needs a vast child-care system. Support for an expanded child-care system comes from diverse groups and is not associated with any particular social ideology. The argument that women with young children should be free to choose between employment and domestic duties and that society is responsible for providing that alternative has received increasing support, especially from women's liberation groups. Those concerned with rising welfare rolls have favored relieving dependent mothers with young children from child-care responsibilities which foreclose labor force participation. Others, focusing on the needs of children, have argued that the home environments of many poor children are not sufficiently attractive or stimulating to prepare them for the demands of primary school. These advocates propose, therefore, that society should provide programs to fill the void.

Since it deals with the foundations of life and bears upon the social fabric, it is not surprising that the provision of child care is clouded by emotionalism, clashes in value systems, and tunnel-vision perspectives. Social concern with parents' care of young children is viewed by some as an invasion of privacy. For others, failure to correct any perceived deficiencies in children's care is equated with lax morality, if not outright crime. The road to hell is paved with good intentions, and in the child-care area, road maps are poorly marked.

1

Child-care programs may serve any of the following three purposes:

1. Child-care programs may facilitate work outside the home and increase family income.

2. Programs may subsidize the costs for mothers who are already in the labor force.

3. Programs may be used to educate and otherwise enhance the health and welfare of children.

These goals are not mutually exclusive, but the design and scope of programs that reflect individual goals or combinations of goals would be quite different, as would their costs.

Many recent arguments for child care have focused on the woman's right to work outside the home. However, it is not certain that a significant proportion of mothers with preschool-age children would enter the labor force if free child-care services were available. The quality of jobs and the level of pay may have more to do with a woman's predisposition to accept employment than does the provision of child care. The fact is that millions of mothers with preschoolers already work and pay for child care out of their earnings. They would be the first in line to take advantage of expanded child-care subsidies. Also, those entering the labor force to take advantage of child-care subsidies probably would have worked anyway. A universal system would probably not improve the competitive position of the marginal worker.

Few can afford to pay directly for all the good things that a day care system might be able to deliver. Highly trained and well-rounded staffs, childproofed buildings with pleasant surroundings, nutritious and well-prepared meals, and medical and social services all add up to an expensive package. Those whose children might benefit most from such services—the poor—can least afford to pay for them.

Issues such as the ratio of children to supervising adults, the credentials of the caretaker, and the structure of the building fall under the major heading of "quality." What should be done for children in addition to keeping them fed, warm, and dry? Believing that the crucial foundations for later learning are laid before children enter the first grade, many urge education as the cure for poverty and other social ills. Therefore, the value of child care is partly measured in direct proportion to educational experiences provided to children. The questions are, then, should there be a universal system, and if so, who should pay for it, and what type of system should it be?

The current child-care "system" is a complex and loosely sewn patchwork reflecting educational goals, subsidies to mothers who already work, and attempts to draw poor mothers into the labor force. Schools, whose primary purpose is education, now enroll increasing proportions of children under six years old, and special publicly supported compensatory programs designed to help children as well as facilitate labor force participation of parents operate outside of the school system. Some mothers dump their children in poorly supervised situations in order to accept employment. Many children are cared for by an informal system of babysitters—friends and relatives who provide care for little or no cost; others are cared for by professional babysitters who charge higher fees. The informal babysitting system, which is relatively low-cost compared with centers and schools, not only facilitates employment of mothers, but also raises family income, given the alternatives of paying for higher-cost care or forgoing employment.

Day care centers and day care homes have developed as alternatives to arrangements with family and friends. Formal centers usually care for six or more children under the supervision of one or more adults in a setting other than the child's home. Programs may be little more than mass babysitting or may include educational and developmental components. Sponsorship is diverse, ranging from institutional do-gooders to profit-motivated entrepreneurs. Private proprietors, labor unions, churches and social agencies, various government programs, and groups of neighborhood mothers all operate child-care centers.

Day care homes, as distinguished from centers, involve a caretaker, usually an adult woman, who supervises a few children for compensation. As with formal day care centers, home arrangements are theoretically subject to state and federal licensing regulations which are observed more in the breach than in their observance. Educated guesses indicate that more than 90 percent of all such homes are in fact unlicensed. Informal babysitting arrangements among neighbors bear striking similarity to day care homes, but neighbors often provide such services as cost-free favors, not regulated by any public authority.

Licensed day care facilities were equipped in 1971 to care for 912,000 children, including 712,000 in day care centers and the balance in day care homes. This capacity would have been sufficient to accommodate one of every six children under age six whose mothers were in the labor force in 1973, assuming that only children of working mothers were cared for in licensed day care centers and that all slots were filled by preschoolers. In practice, however, children of single male family heads, nonworking mothers, and school-age children are also enrolled in licensed day care facilities.

Most working mothers depend therefore on conventional child-care arrangements. In well-to-do families, housekeepers or maids may be hired to care for children in the home. But, with the rising cost of private household workers, this option is available to a declining proportion of the highest earners. In-home babysitters may be hired at less expense. Supervision of youngsters when mother works remains largely a family function provided by fathers, sisters, or grandmothers. Mothers in flexible job arrangements may take children to work with them. Such situations are largely limited to mom-and-pop businesses, farm work, and domestic jobs. A substantial number are "latchkey children" (children who have a key to the house) who look after themselves until parents return. Although most latchkey children are of school age and are unattended for brief periods, preschool-age children are also too frequently left on their own.

In 1973, there were 19.1 million children under six years old, of whom 6.0 million had working mothers. Forty-four percent of all three- to five-year-olds attended nursery schools or kindergartens, and two of every three of these children were in publicly supported institutions, including Head Start and similar preschool education programs. Since schools for young children usually offer services for only part of the working day, other child-care arrangements are needed to supplement them. In addition, over half of working mothers with preschool-age children had children under three years old for whom institutional care arrangements were almost completely lacking.

About 700,000 children are cared for in day care centers, of which half are run by public and voluntary organizations and half are proprietary enterprises. Sample studies suggest that about one-fourth of day care centers offer custodial care only, half offer some educational benefits, and one-fourth offer a full range of developmental services. Since some center slots serve children with nonworking parents and some serve children over six years old, fewer than 10 percent of preschool-age children of working mothers are cared for in centers. In addition, some of these centers are primarily educational and are also counted as preschool programs.

Care in a home—the child's own or that of a babysitter or relative—makes up the bulk of child care. Relatives provide about two-fifths of this care, nonrelatives the rest. Such in-home arrangements are primarily custodial and are compatible with the mother's employment and the pocketbook, but they may not satisfy children's educational needs. Nevertheless, considering that many of the caregivers are relatives and close friends, care may be similar to that which would be provided by the mother. Also, many arrangements supplement a preprimary school program.

Federal programs do a little of everything: Federal child-care dollars primarily facilitate employment of marginal earners and welfare recipients. In addition, small but increasing subsidies are made to working mothers through tax provisions to partially cover the cost of child care, and an increasing variety of preprimary education programs receive federal support. Recent trends suggest that the federal child-care role will expand to include increasing proportions of children from poor as well as more affluent homes.

CHAPTER TWO / WORKING MOTHERS

The sex composition of the work force has been constantly changing since World War II. Females, including mothers, are entering the labor force in increasing numbers, while men are dropping out. In 1940, a little over one-fourth of the female population over fourteen years old worked, but only 30 percent of the working women were "married with husbands present," to use the phrase of the official government counters. World War II labor shortages drew women, both married and unmarried, into the labor force, boosting the participation rate of women. After the war, women apparently retained their taste for outside occupations.

Between 1950 and 1973, the civilian labor force increased by 26.5 million persons, and women accounted for three-fifths of this growth (chart 1). Altogether, the 34 million women in the labor force made up nearly two-fifths of all workers. But women were more prone to work part time: nearly three of every ten working women were on part-time schedules, compared to one in ten working men. The best available projections anticipate a continued rise in the female labor force participation rate.

An outstanding trend over the last decade was the increased labor force participation of mothers with preschool-age children. In 1973, one in three ✳ mothers with preschool children worked, and one in five worked full time. One decade earlier, less than one in four worked, and only one in seven worked full time. Altogether, 4.4 million mothers of preschool-age children were working in March 1973 (table 1).

5

CHILDREN OF WORKING MOTHERS

Data on children with working mothers have been available only since 1970. During the subsequent three years the total number of children below age six years declined by half a million, but the number living in two-parent households declined by one million and the number living

CHART 1. The labor force participation rate has risen for women, but declined for men.

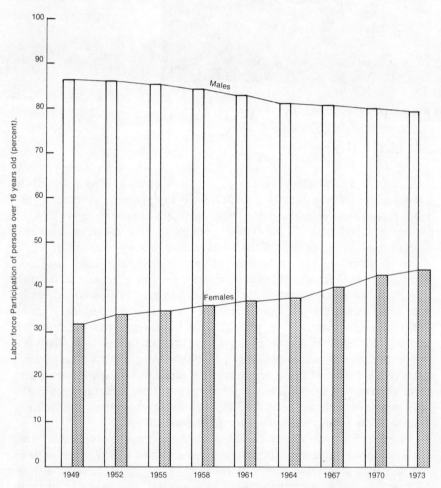

Source: *Manpower Report of the President, 1974* (Washington: Government Printing Office, 1974), Tables A-3, A-4.

TABLE 1. Mothers with preschool-age children, 1973 (in thousands).

	Total	Percent	Wives	Percent	Divorced, separated, widowed	Percent
TOTAL	13,914	100.0	12,394	100.0	1,520	100.0
Labor Force	4,764	34.2	4,056	32.7	708	46.6
Employed	4,398	31.6	3,787	30.5	611	40.2
Full time	2,929	21.0	2,461	19.9	465	30.6
Part time	1,391	10.0	1,251	10.1	143	9.4
Agriculture	78	.6	75	.6	3	.2
Unemployed	366	2.6	269	2.4	97	6.4

Source: Howard Hayghe, "Marital and Family Characteristics of the Labor Force in March 1973," U.S. Bureau of Labor Statistics, Special Labor Force Report No. 164, p. 20.

in female-headed households rose by half a million (table 2). These developments affected labor force participation as the number of working mothers increased, especially in families headed by women.

Preschool-age children with working mothers

	1973	Percent change since 1970
Total	5,952,000	+ 6.5
Two-parent families	5,097,000	+ 3.0
Female-headed families	885,000	+ 33.0

About two-fifths of all preschool-age children living in female-headed families have working mothers. However, the proportion of such white preschoolers with working mothers increased in recent years while the proportion of such black preschoolers with working mothers declined.

If the birth rate continues to decline or remains at the low levels of the 1970s, the prospect is that the number of preschool-age children with working mothers will stabilize and may even decline, although the percentage with working mothers may continue to increase. Rising labor force participation of mothers in two-parent families has the greatest potential for growth. If the divorce and illegitimacy rates continue to climb, the number of children with working mothers will also increase.

The 1972 annual income of female-headed families with preschool-age children was $4,600 if the mother worked but only $2,700 if the mother was out of the labor force. In comparison, the median family income of children in two-parent families was $11,000, and it was $12,000 if their mothers

TABLE 2. Although the total number of preschool-age children declined, children in single-parent households increased between 1970 and 1973.

	1973 (in thousands)	Percent change since 1970
Total children under 6 years	19,145	− 2.4%
White	16,416	− 3.0
Black	2,400	+ .8
In husband-wife families	16,905	− 5.7
White	15,211	− 4.8
Black	1,419	−15.7
In female-headed families	2,149	+34.9
White	1,149	+26.5
Black	950	+43.3
Other male family heads	91	− 2.3

Source: U.S. Bureau of Labor Statistics, Summary/Special Labor Force Report, "Children of Working Mothers, March 1973," September 1973, p. 4.

worked. Clearly, children in families headed by women experience lower living standards than those in two-parent families, even if their mothers do work: many of these children are being raised in severe poverty.

WHO ARE THE WORKING MOTHERS?

Young mothers work for a number of reasons, the same as men. Married women may contribute a major portion of the family income or they may supplement their husbands' incomes. Women without husbands may be the sole support of their families. Other women may simply shun housework and prefer cash for their work. The incentives to work and the opportunities to do so vary according to marital status, income of the husband, presence and age of children, educational level, age, and race. Combinations of these factors plus work opportunities in the area of residence largely dictate whether women's time will be spent homemaking or wage earning. Divorced, separated, and widowed women had higher labor force participation rates than their married counterparts, reflecting increased financial responsibilities (chart 2). Divorced women have the highest labor force participation rates of all categories of women, including that of single women.

Age and education are strong predictors of labor force participation. However, these variables cannot be considered in isolation from marital status. The rate of labor force participation for women with young children positively correlates with educational attainment. Rising educational attainment of women exercises an upward push in labor force participation because women acquire salable skills and the incentive to use them (table 3). The presence in the home of children aged six years or less reduces the likelihood that their mothers will work. However, proportionately more college-educated women tend to work while raising young children, and more return to the labor market as their children reach school age.

Increasing availability of part-time jobs has also enticed many young mothers into the labor force who would not have worked full time. Between

CHART 2. Married women are less likely to work than single women, 1973.

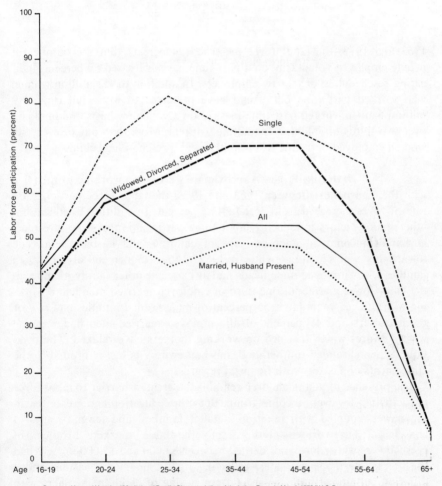

Source: Howard Hayghe, "Marital and Family Characteristics of the Labor Force in March 1973," U.S. Bureau of Labor Statistics, Special Labor Force Report, No. 164, Table B.

TABLE 3. Labor force participation of married women by education and age of children, March 1973.

Education of women	No children under 18	Children 16 to 17	Children under 6
TOTAL	42.8%	50.1%	32.7%
Less than 4 years of high school	27.9	43.9	28.4
4 years of high school	50.6	52.5	33.1
4 years or more of college	66.0	57.7	39.1

Source: Howard Hayghe, "Marital and Family Characteristics of the Labor Force in March 1973," U.S. Bureau of Labor Statistics, Special Labor Force Report No. 164, Table P.

1963 and 1973, the labor force increased 24 percent, but the number of people employed voluntarily on a part-time basis increased 51 percent, indicating rescheduling of jobs by employers. In addition to 1.2 million women who worked part time but would have preferred to work full time, 7.9 million women worked part time in 1973 on a voluntary basis and made up over two-thirds of voluntary part-time workers. More than one of every six women employed part time was a mother of a preschool-age child.

Working Wives. Approximately six in ten working women live with their husbands. Between 1963 and 1973, the labor force participation rate of wives increased from 36.1 to 42.2 percent. In addition to education, other major factors influencing labor force participation of wives are race, husband's income, number and age of children, and husband's attitude toward his wife's employment. In 1962, about 45 percent of American families with employed male heads had at least one other family member in the labor force, and about one-third of employed married men had a working wife. Eleven years later, 55 percent of male-headed families had two or more earners and 45 percent of all employed married men had working wives.[1] Mores which frowned on working mothers have relaxed. The mystique which shrouded motherhood and housewifery is losing ground to the enticements of a career with financial rewards.

The presence of young children remains the greatest barrier to labor force participation for every income group. But more education and greater earning power, coupled with inflation, smaller families, and fewer twinges of conscience, have drawn mothers into the labor market. Mothers of preschoolers whose husbands earned between $3,000 and $5,000 in 1972 had the highest participation rates, reflecting tight economic situations and a differing cultural attitude on the proper raising of children. Mothers with

TABLE 4. Earnings of the husband influence participation rates of married women differently according to the ages of their children.

| | Participation rates of wives with children by age | | | | | |
| | 1961 | | 1967 | | 1973 | |
Husband's earnings in the previous year	Below 6 years	6 to 18 years	Below 6 years	6 to 18 years	Below 6 years	6 to 18 years
TOTAL	20.0%	41.7%	26.5%	45.0%	32.7%	50.1%
Under $3,000	26.7	50.4	32.0	49.5	44.6	50.9
$3,000–$4,999	25.0	48.4	34.4	52.0	35.7	55.4
$5,000–$6,999	17.5	41.1	31.6	49.9	38.6	57.1
$7,000–$9,999	10.1	30.4	19.5	40.5	37.8	56.8
$10,000 and over					26.3	46.1

Source: Jacob Schiffman, "Marital and Family Characteristics of Workers, March 1961," U.S. Bureau of Labor Statistics, Special Labor Force Report No. 20, Table L; Elizabeth Waldman, "Marital and Family Status of Workers, March 1967," U.S. Bureau of Labor Statistics, Special Labor Force Report No. 94, Table J; Howard Hayghe, "Marital and Family Characteristics of the Labor Force in March 1973," U.S. Bureau of Labor Statistics, Special Labor Force Report No. 164, Table J.

older children had the greatest tendency to work if their husbands earned between $5,000 and $7,000. After that point, participation rates declined, but not perceptibly until earnings exceeded $10,000 annually (table 4).

However, the bulk of working wives with preschool-age children do not fit the economic hardship prototype. Although women married to low earners had the highest labor force participation of any income group, only a relatively small fraction of all working wives were married to men earning less than $5,000 a year in 1972.

Annual earnings of husbands in 1972	*Wives in the labor force with preschool-age children, 1973*
Total	100%
Under $5,000	16
$5,000 to $9,999	47
$10,000 or more	37

Women married to low earners have more compelling reasons to work, but they also tend to have built-in disadvantages which limit their chances for constant gainful employment. The likelihood of being saddled with inadequate education, large families, health problems, and residence in low-income areas with limited job opportunities is greater.

Poor wives had higher participation rates than more affluent women in 1961, but the rate for higher income groups is rapidly catching up. The comparative growth of participation rates suggests that work opportunities among the poorest group may have reached full potential, with additional gains limited by educational and health deficiencies, family responsibilities, and other factors. Public income support programs may have diminished work incentives, especially among women with preschool-age children. Higher income groups have more potential for expanding labor force participation, and future gains can be expected among these women.

Wives of unemployed family heads have more compelling financial reasons to enter the labor force, with 48 percent in the labor force as opposed to 41.5 percent of all wives in 1971. Wives of unemployed husbands are also likely to experience higher than average unemployment rates. However, the presence of the wife in the labor force raised family income of households with unemployed male heads 44 percent in 1970.[2]

On an overall basis, wives' propensity to enter the labor force increased when their earnings meant the difference between living close to the low-income threshold or living at a middle-income standard. Once the husband's earnings passed the $10,000 mark, labor force participation of young mothers dropped perceptibly. Black wives with preschool-age children are an exception. Their labor force participation was highest when their husbands earned $10,000 or more a year, probably reflecting high educational attainment and drive for upward mobility.

Recent income maintenance experiments tested the impact of a guaranteed income on labor force attachment of low-income husband-wife families. The guaranteed income grant ranged from 50 to 125 percent of the poverty income line. Additional earnings reduced the basic grant by varying implicit tax rates ranging from 30 to 70 percent. Findings indicated the grant had little impact on labor force participation of males, but it significantly reduced the labor force participation of white wives. Labor force participation of nonwhite wives was unchanged even though the sample was matched for family size and age of children and many large families with young children were included.[3] Apparently, the increased income did not weaken the labor force attachment of nonwhite wives.

The child's age influences the working patterns of mothers more than any other single factor. For all wives with husbands present, the presence of children under three years old had the greatest impact upon curtailing labor force participation, with a second jump in employment occurring when children reach six years (table 5). The increased propensity of mothers to join the labor force after young children pass preschool age has been verified by a longitudinal study which found that the labor force participation of thirty- to forty-four-year-old mothers with children who were under

TABLE 5. The age of children strongly influences labor force participation rates of married women.

		Labor force participation rates			
		Wives with children under 18 years old			
Year	All wives	Total	6–18	3–5	0–3
1960	30.3%	27.6%	39.0%	25.1%	15.3%
1963	33.7	31.2	41.5	28.5	19.4
1966	35.4	33.2	43.7	29.1	21.2
1969	39.6	38.6	48.6	34.7	24.2
1972	41.5	40.5	50.2	36.1	26.9
1973	42.2	41.7	50.1	38.8	29.4

Source: U.S. Bureau of Labor Statistics, Summary/Special Labor Force Report, "Marital and Family Characteristics of the Labor Force in March 1973," and Special Labor Force Report No. 164, p. 22.

six years old in 1967 but older than six years in 1969 rose by 7 percent. However, transition into the labor force at this stage of family maturation was associated solely with wives of white-collar workers. Conversely, one in ten white wives who had no preschoolers in 1967 but who had one in 1969 dropped out of the labor force. These patterns reflect cultural norms dictating child-rearing practices and suggest that increased availability of subsidized quality day care would effect greater increases in the labor force participation of women of more affluent families than that of other groups.[4]

Although a smaller percentage of women with preschool-age children are in the labor force at any one time, almost half of married women with three- to five-year-old children and 43 percent of mothers with children under three years old had some work experience in 1972.

The number of children in the family affects whether or not the mother works. About two-fifths of wives with only one preschool-age child worked in 1973, compared to less than one-fourth of women with two or more children.[5] Multiple child households do not necessarily deter labor force participation of the mother if one or more siblings are old enough to look after themselves and younger children. Child care provided by a teenage brother or sister is the cheapest available and is often used by low-income mothers.

The presence and age of children influences not only the decision to work, but also the choice of full-time or part-time employment. In 1973, over three in ten women with preschoolers worked, and almost two in ten worked full time.[6]

The presence of young children also may hamper the ability to find a suitable job or may cause women to be more selective in the jobs they take. The 1973 unemployment rate among married women with children under six years was 7.7 percent, three-fifths higher than the rate for women with older children. Young children may not only limit job choices acceptable to mothers but may also discourage prospective employers from hiring mothers. Jobs which are too distant, rigidly scheduled, or time-consuming may conflict too greatly with family responsibilities.

Attitudes toward Working Wives and Mothers. A wife's perception of her husband's attitude toward working wives influences her labor force participation, but it has more influence in white families than in black. Also, wives may be influenced more by the norm for their social subgroup than by the attitude of their husbands. Three-fifths of black husbands had favorable attitudes toward wives working, while only one-fifth of white husbands felt the same. White wives perceiving favorable attitudes worked an average of thirty-three weeks in 1967, compared to nine weeks worked by wives who perceived a veto message on the idea. The husband's attitude in black families apparently had a lesser impact. Black wives perceiving positive attitudes by their husbands worked an average of thirty-four weeks, as opposed to twenty weeks worked by those whose husbands disapproved.[7]

Changing Patterns in Family Formation and Size. Undoubtedly, careers are playing increasingly important roles in women's lives. Several other social trends simultaneously facilitate and reinforce the inclinations of women to work. These include delaying marriage, deferring first births, and preference for smaller family size. Two-fifths of twenty- to twenty-four-year-old women were single in 1973, compared to less than three in ten in 1960.[8] Family size preferences and the age at which a woman bears her first child have also changed. In 1960, eighteen- to twenty-four-year-old wives averaged 1.4 children and expected a total of 3.1 births. In 1973, wives in this age cohort averaged 0.9 births and expected a total of 2.3 births.[9] These patterns accommodate longer education and greater career development. Consequently, more women are remaining in the labor force after children are born. Of those who drop out of the labor force, higher percentages are returning even before their children reach school age.

Is There a "Typical" Working Wife? Working wives with children under six years old fit no single prototype. There are some whose economic contribution is essential for family survival, but these are a minority. Much employment reflects the augmentation of family income for "extras." Almost half of all young married mothers are at least intermittently employed. Some women return to the labor force or remain employed after the birth of a child only to find that the combined burdens of a job and small children are too much to carry or that the job is less stimulating or less remunerative than anticipated, when child-care costs are considered. When adequate sources of support are already available, wives are free to move in and out of the labor force without serious economic repercussions.

An increasing proportion of young married women remain in the labor force after the arrival of children in order to follow careers. Although labor force participation of college-educated mothers decreases as husbands' earnings increase, more continue to work regardless of their husbands' incomes. Current trends suggest that the middle-class family will be smaller and better planned to accommodate career ambitions of both husband and wife. Increasing proportions of mothers will work even though there are no pressing financial needs. Accordingly, these families will be increasingly affluent.

FEMALE HEADS OF HOUSEHOLDS

Economic and labor force problems are far more severe for mothers who have no husbands to support them. The increases in divorce, separation, desertion, and illegitimacy have swelled the number of female-headed households with young children. The American marriage contract is becoming increasingly short-term. In 1960, there were forty-two divorced women for every thousand intact marriages, and 1.5 percent of all married couples were separated. In 1972, there were sixty-six divorced women for every thousand marriages, and the separation rate increased to 2.6 percent of all marriages. Marriage instability dramatically increased the population of families headed by women. In 1962, 450,000 women with preschool-age children were without husbands, but in 1973, 708,000 women were in this situation. Altogether, 2.1 million children under six years old lived in these families. Half of the children were white and half were from minority races.

There is some evidence that the rise in female-headed households may tend to exaggerate the incidence of unstable families. One study estimated that 38 percent of the 1.6 million increase in female family heads between 1940 and 1970 was due to the higher propensity to form separate households instead of combining with other family members; 18 percent was due to population increase; 7 percent was due to the increase in the proportion of women having at least one child; and the interaction of these factors accounted for 90 percent of the increase in female-headed families. Increased marital disruption in combination with other factors accounted for the remaining 10 percent.[10] Another study found that illegitimacy and marital disruption accounted for about one-third the increase in female family heads. Population increases, declining incidence of childless women, and other factors accounted for the rest.[11]

These two studies suggest that availability of outside income, either through transfers or work efforts, allows a greater proportion of husbandless mothers to form independent households. Without support mechanisms, they would presumably have combined with relatives and formed family units which may or may not have been headed by women.

Observers disagree on what proportion of female-headed families result from increased illegitimacy and marital disruption. It appears that the incidence has increased rapidly in recent years. What is more controversial is whether alternative sources of support, albeit marginal ones, such as AFDC or employment, have contributed to marital disruption.

Women who head families experience multiple problems. Disproportionate numbers live in poverty. One-third of female-headed families were below the poverty threshold in 1972, compared to 6 percent of male-headed families. A greater proportion of husbandless mothers have large families; 11 percent had four or more children, compared to 8 percent of two-parent families in 1972. Fewer are well educated. Forty-six percent of female family heads under forty-five years old had not completed high school, compared to 22 percent of the total female population between eighteen and forty-five years of age. Lower educational achievement prevents some from obtaining employment and relegates many more to lower paying jobs. Larger proportions are minority race women. Blacks comprise one-third of female-headed families with children but only 9 percent of all two-parent families.

As is the case in two-parent households, the age of children affects the mother's labor force participation. Although three-fifths of husbandless mothers with children under eighteen years old were in the labor force in 1973, over two-thirds of female family heads with children between six and seventeen years old were in the labor force, compared to less than half of mothers with children under six years old.

The age of the children also affects the incidence of unemployment and the percentage of mothers who work part time. The unemployment rate is higher for single mothers, especially when preschoolers are part of the household—12.5 percent of whites and 22.0 percent of black single mothers of preschoolers were unemployed in 1973. For women with older children unemployment was half that rate, but it was still above the comparable rates for women in two-parent families. The higher levels of unemployment reflect increased pressures for these family heads to enter the labor market, their greater child rearing responsibilities, and in many cases, poor educational preparation.

The number and age of children combined with race also affects labor force participation. Although the number of children in female-headed families averaged 2.2—the same as two-parent families—the distribution of children in female-headed families is skewed toward the extremes. More of these women have either one child or more than four children. Two-thirds of those with only one child were in the labor force in 1973, compared to less than half of single mothers with three or more children under eighteen years old.

The larger the family, the greater the probability that the mother is poorly educated, out of the work force, and that the family lives in poverty. In 1973, 54 percent of women who headed families with children under six years old were not in the labor force, and this group of families included almost three-fifths of the preschool-age children in female-headed households. The annual income of these families averaged $2,700 in 1972. It is apparent that the majority of these mothers and children lived in poverty.

WOMEN NOT IN THE
LABOR FORCE

While women have joined the labor force in large numbers, 42.7 million of the 77.2 million women who were over sixteen years of age in 1973 did not seek work outside the home. They cited family responsibilities, school attendance, ill health, old age and retirement, inability to get a job, and other reasons for nonparticipation in the labor force. The primary reason varies with the age of the respondent, with teenagers reporting school attendance and older women reporting ill health and retirement most frequently. Five of every six women aged twenty to fifty-nine years cited family as the reason for not working. One in twenty indicated that she would be willing to work if a job were available.[12]

Apparently, most women who want to work are in fact in the labor force. Some are prevented from working by family responsibilities; however, these responsibilities are not necessarily relieved by day care services. According to a U.S. Department of Labor survey, only 12 percent of women who wanted jobs and 1 percent of women who were out of the labor force would have joined the labor force if acceptable child care arrangements had been available.[13] Child care accounts for only part of the need. Many women may feel that young children need their mother's care in the home regardless of the availability of surrogate-care alternatives. But the preference for home responsibility may be modified by the wages the mother could command and the costs of the services she would be unable to render in the home, including child-care costs. Perceptions of family responsibility may also change over time through educational attainment, reduced family size, and the establishment of institutions which provide family services.

THE SPECIAL CASE—THE
AFDC POPULATION

Federal policy has long recognized the economic hardships of mothers who are sole providers for their families. Starting with the 1935 Social Security Act, special programs, including death and disability insurance and public assistance, were instituted to provide income supports and other services. Aid to dependent children was designed to mitigate the need of widowed, divorced, and husbandless mothers to leave their children in another's care in order to work. It was anticipated that, with the expanded coverage of social security insurance provisions, the need for public assistance, especially for widowed mothers, would wither away. However, due to social changes, the envisioned recipients—widowed mothers or wives of incapacitated men—made up a decreasing proportion of the supported population, while the proportion of mothers who were divorced, deserted, or never married increased.

Welfare is an alternative to work. The practical results are that the number of families supported on AFDC rolls tripled between 1961 and 1973, reaching 7.6 million children in 3.0 million families. One-third of the families had at least one child under three years old, and the same proportion had a three- to five-year-old child. Altogether, 2.6 million children under the age six lived in families supported by AFDC. The current AFDC population is predominantly headed by young single mothers.

Changing family structures have affected the burgeoning AFDC caseload. Families headed by women are prime candidates for public assistance, and while the percentage of such families has increased for the total population, this has been especially true among black households. One in every ten white families was headed by a woman in 1973, compared with one in every three black families (chart 3). In 1971, more than half of black female-headed families received public assistance, as did one in five white families headed by women.

Several trends are discernible. The increase in the proportion of families headed by females, coupled with the rise in AFDC-supported female-headed families, indicates that availability of support affords women the opportunity to form separate family units. Though the argument that availability of AFDC contributes to the formation of husbandless families is not proven, it does appear to be supported by data. Criteria for eligibility certainly militate against marriage, especially if the father is a marginal earner. Women accept welfare because work alternatives are not very attractive. Although emphasis on longer education has resulted in rising levels of educational attainment among AFDC mothers, they remain educationally handicapped compared to the rest of the population. Consequently, their occupational choices are limited, and those who do work are

CHART 3. Growing proportions of families are headed by women.

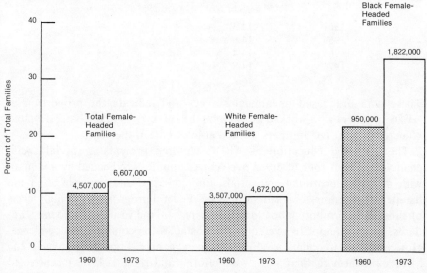

Source: U.S. Bureau of the Census, *Statistical Abstract of the United States, 1971* (Washington: Government Printing Office, 1971), p. 37; and "Households and Families, by Type: March 1973," Series P-20, No. 251, June 1973, Table 2.

concentrated in low-skill, low-paying jobs. While the poor may want to work, the availability of alternative support makes low-paying menial occupations the less attractive option.

Work Incentives. To induce AFDC recipients to work, the federal law provides that work expenses and the first $30 of monthly earnings plus one-third of the balance can be disregarded in computing welfare benefits. In addition, numerous support services are provided to enable the family head to work.

In practice, the amount of earnings which a worker can keep varies from state to state. The marginal tax rate on earnings is a function of the liberality and ingenuity of the caseworker, and the actual work incentive generously exceeds the amount legislated in a substantial number of cases.[14] In some instances the disregarded income exceeds the reach of most AFDC recipients. A 1971 GAO report indicated that an AFDC mother with three children in Los Angeles could earn $579 a month before AFDC grants were reduced and $1,074 a month before benefits were terminated.[15]

Coupled with these positive incentives is the requirement that AFDC adults participate in work training or employment unless exempted for good cause. Those who are not exempted from participation but refuse to accept training or employment may forfeit benefits. As the relatively stable percentage of employed AFDC mothers attests, these efforts have borne only marginal results:[16]

1961	14.3%
1967	14.8
1969	14.4
1971	14.8
1973	16.2

These data are based on annual surveys and indicate the proportion of AFDC mothers who worked at the time the survey was taken. An estimated 40 percent of AFDC mothers worked at least part of the year.[17]

The care and education of AFDC children presents a special social challenge. About four of every five AFDC families are headed by a woman with meager educational credentials, limited skills, and multiple other job handicaps impeding total self-sufficiency. Federal programs offer high levels of support to promote labor force participation and to improve living standards, in an attempt to overcome the obstacles to economic independence. However, too frequently, AFDC mothers cannot hope to purchase the "free" aid through their own work efforts, and there is little incentive to terminate dependence completely.

Many of the support programs concern the needs of children in the family. In order to work, mothers have to have an alternative child-care arrangement. Often, counseling is needed in order to maintain the family unit and to assist mothers in coping with their multiple responsibilities. The children may need alternative sources of guidance and tutoring because the parent is incapable of providing the help.

Children living in AFDC families suffer economic and attendant educational disadvantages. They are more likely than other children to acquire educational and occupational handicaps and to experience poverty and dependency in adulthood. Public programs have been developed to compensate these children for alleged privations in their home lives. Some compensatory programs have also attempted to promote employment of parents. While lack of income is a direct result of lack of employment, programs for the children may have little impact on the parents' employability and perhaps should be judged for their impact on children rather than on parents' employability.

THE NEED FOR NEW ARRANGEMENTS

The trend of mothers to join the labor force and remain in it seems irreversible. Women's occupational status is improving and their earning power is increasing, but they remain at a competitive work disadvantage. Their responsibilities remain split between work and homes and children, despite the fact that deferred marriages, reduced family size, and labor-saving household gadgetry have diminished domestic demands.

Equal employment opportunity, utilization of full potential, and economic equality with men will not solve the problems of single mothers. In addition to being the sole breadwinner, they tend to be limited by education and training deficiencies and other work impediments. Even when employed at full potential, many single mothers will need supplementary support.

Society is depending more on the work of mothers, and increasing numbers of children are dependent only on their mothers for support. This calls for new institutional arrangements for unattended children in order to fill the void created by working mothers. Most single mothers and many two-parent families are not able to pay for the care, and the case for selective public support of child-care facilities is receiving increasing attention.

This generally recognized problem raises other questions. Should mothers who are marginal earners be encouraged to work in the marketplace rather than care for their own children? Should society provide special recognition of work-related child-care expenses of wives in light of higher taxes paid on additional income? Who then should receive child-care subsidies? These questions involve deep emotional values, and cost-benefit ratios are of little help in establishing guidelines for action.

The acceptance of new institutional arrangements for child care leaves unresolved many issues dealing with implementation. Should help be confined to direct and indirect financial assistance for the child-care arrangement of the parent's choice using vouchers or tax credits, or should choices be regulated by public provision of certain types of centers? An examination of the ways working mothers currently care for their children, their satisfaction and preferences, and the amount women are willing to pay provides clues to what the customer wants and what government should provide.

CHAPTER THREE / HOW DO
WORKING MOTHERS CARE FOR
THEIR CHILDREN?

FACTORS AFFECTING
CHILD CARE

Working mothers are no new phenomenon in America, and surrogate child-care arrangements do not represent a radical departure from family life. Mothers have tapped various alternatives, from available grandmas to organized group situations, while supplementing the family income or earning the entire family living. The major change in the past two decades has been one of magnitude.

Alternate care for the children of working mothers and for children whose mothers are out shopping or doing other chores runs the gamut from formal centers to dependence upon latch keys till mom gets home. Traditionally, family members or trusted neighbors watched children during their mother's absence. Modern American families are more geographically mobile than in previous eras, which has led to the breakup of extended families and close neighborhood ties. American nuclear families are more isolated than ever before. Perhaps traditional child-care arrangements have become inadequate in meeting working mothers' needs, not because they are less desirable, but because there are not enough to go around.

Child-care arrangements outside the home have been slowly assuming the

22

roles of family members.[1] The supply of grandmas and aunties willing to take young children all day evidently did not keep pace with the number of full-time working mothers, partly because the supply dwindled as many of the babysitters took on full-time jobs themselves.

In-home care by babysitters or housekeepers is relatively infrequent. Few can afford to hire a housekeeper or maid, and the practice is still disproportionately concentrated in the South, where a low wage labor supply persists. However, even there it is a disappearing luxury, as 1974 minimum wage extensions covered domestic help for the first time and pushed the cost beyond the means of all but the affluent.

Babysitting in the child's home is more associated with after-school care. Although many working mothers prefer to have someone in the house while they are away, out-of-home babysitters are being increasingly used for care of preschool-age children. The Ohio State University Center for Human Resource Research studies reported that close to one-fourth of thirty- to forty-four-year-old working mothers used family day care homes in 1967. Among younger women, aged fourteen to twenty-four years, almost two-fifths of working mothers who made child care arrangements used out-of-home babysitters in 1968.

As mothers of younger children have entered the labor force, they seem to have turned to out-of-home babysitters to a much greater extent, probably because they were the most preferable available option. With limitations on the number of willing grandmas, and constraints on the availability of group care centers—due to limited slots, undesirability, or excessive cost—the expansion seems to have occurred most among informal day care homes—the network of "women who take care of children."[2]

Relatives provide about half of all care for preschool-age children while their mothers work, and half of that care is provided in the child's own home. In low-income families, care in the home by family members is even more common. About three in ten children are cared for by nonrelatives, and roughly a third of this care is provided in the child's home and the rest in the caretaker's home. Fewer than one child in ten is cared for in a center. The balance are cared for by their mothers while working, are left to take care of themselves, or are in some other unspecified arrangement (chart 4).

Child-care arrangements vary according to a mother's working hours, marital status, race, the age and number of children, presence of other adults or older children in the home, and family income.

1. PART-TIME WORK. Mothers who work part time tend to make significantly different child-care arrangements than do full-time workers in that the former seldom go outside the family for care. One-fourth of part-time women workers scheduled employment only while their children were in school. Of those with conflicting work schedules, nine out of ten arrange-

CHART 4. According to recent surveys, most work-related child care is in the home and by relatives.

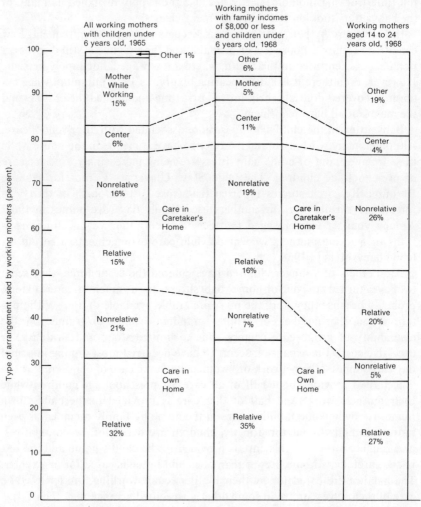

Note: Percentages do not add to 100 because of rounding.

Source: Seth Low and Pearl G. Spindler, *Child Care Arrangements of Working Mothers in the United States* (Washington: Government Printing Office, 1968), p. 71; Westinghouse Learning Corporation and Westat Research, *Day Care Survey 1970—Summary Report and Basic Analysis* (Rockville, Md.: Westinghouse Learning Corporation and Westat Research, 1971), pp. 177-178; John R. Shea, Roger D. Roderick, Frederick A. Zeller, Andrew I. Kohen and Associates, *Years for Decision: A Longitudinal Study of the Educational and Labor Market Experience of Young Women*, Vol. 1 (Columbus, Ohio: Ohio State University Center for Human Resource Research, 1971), p. 138.

ments involved family members and almost two-fifths of these arrangements involved the mother looking after her children while working.

2. MARITAL STATUS. Fathers provided child care for 15 to 20 percent of married women who work. Female heads of households do not have this alternative and rely on other family members living in the home to a much greater extent. Problems in acquiring child care were more severe for single mothers, and limitations in economic resources were reflected in their choice of care by relatives. Compared to other working mothers, single mothers were twice as likely to arrange for in-home care by relatives under sixteen years.[3]

3. AGE OF CHILDREN. The services needed and the suitable options for obtaining them vary with the child's age. Group facilities usually limit enrollment to children aged three to five years. Licensing regulations in ten states prohibit care of children under two and a half years old in group centers and twelve other states require that special conditions be met.[4] The demands of very young children often preclude working and watching children at the same time.

Since children above the age of six years are under the supervision of a school system for six or seven hours a day, child-care needs are different. Older children have fewer unsupervised hours and are more able to take care of themselves, so working mothers make arrangements accordingly.

4. NUMBER OF CHILDREN IN THE FAMILY. The number of children in the family influences not only the mother's decision to work but also her choice of child-care arrangements. Out-of-home care arrangements for more than one child frequently require multiple arrangements and multiplied expense. For these reasons, working women with a number of children are far more likely to make in-home arrangements, often using older children to help supervise younger ones. The pattern of child-care arrangements in families with more than two children has definite implications for future demand. As fertility rates decline, the number of working mothers with only one or two children will increase. Since one- or two-child families tend to favor out-of-home care, the demand for this type of care is likely to increase. It is, however, impossible to predict whether the demand will be for regulated or unregulated child care.

5. RACIAL PATTERNS. There are also distinct racial patterns in child care. The higher incidence of female-headed families among blacks requires more black mothers to provide child care without the help of a husband. Black mothers tend, therefore, to depend upon relatives for child-care arrangements more than white mothers do. Black mothers also tend to use day care centers to a greater extent. One survey found that 15 percent of black mothers, compared to only 4 percent of white mothers, use day care centers. Differential use of centers by race may be accounted for by several

variables. Parents struggling for upward mobility place greater emphasis on early education, and many feel that day care centers offer this. A large proportion of the centers run by church, social, and public agencies that have developed since 1965 are urban and serve predominantly black communities. Centers, especially subsidized or low-cost centers, are less frequent in white suburbia. Also, middle-class whites are more prone to associate centers with "undesirable influences" or doubt the ability of day care centers to provide healthy or beneficial child-rearing situations.[5]

ATTITUDES TOWARD CHILD-CARE ARRANGEMENTS

Many working mothers perceive the arrangements made for their children as less than satisfactory, and the reported incidence of misgivings probably belies the true level of dissatisfaction. Mothers may underreport unsatisfactory child care because of rationalization, inhibition, or guilt.[6] About one in ten working mothers indicated strong misgivings about the child-care provisions made for their children, and an additional four in ten stated that the arrangements did not meet with their full approval. Also, dissatisfaction seems more common among low-income families.

Dissatisfaction was associated with all types of care arrangements, whether at home or in a center. Fear of inadequate supervision was a common complaint, but imposition on relatives, inconvenient locations, time constraints, and the expense incurred in child-care arrangements also contributed to discontent. The most satisfactory arrangements were in-home care by relatives other than siblings and care in group centers. Although day care centers appear to be more popular than other types of care, their use is contingent on the quality and cost of the care they provide, the location of the center, and the availability of other low-cost and convenient alternatives.

A mother's dissatisfaction with child-care arrangements may reflect the caretaker's orientation and philosophy rather than the "quality" of care offered. For instance, some mothers may object to the lax discipline while others using an identical facility may feel discipline is too strict. Some may favor free play for preschoolers while others want their children to learn the ABCs. Other mothers prefer an in-home arrangement and would be dissatisfied with any outside arrangement, even if it were offered free. Some reject surrogate care altogether and would like to care for the children themselves, but this approach would presumably require giving up work.

Preferences in Child-Care Arrangements. Parents' preferences for alternatives to present child-care arrangements present a clearer picture of attitudes. Several surveys of both nonworking and working mothers have explored this issue. A 1962 Child Welfare League study of working and nonworking women with children under twelve years old found that 47 percent of mothers would use day care centers if they were available. The study described a hypothetical center resembling a nursery school operated by a community or social agency, with children under the supervision of teachers, and asked respondents to indicate their reaction to such a center. Mothers on the lower end of the economic spectrum showed the highest level of interest in such centers and blacks were more receptive than whites to the idea. The study also showed that the appeal of day care centers depended on local experience. If local facilities were closely associated with what the study termed "problem populations," enthusiasm for broadening such services was dampened.[7]

Another report studied changes in day care arrangements desired by low- to middle-income working mothers with preschool-age children.[8] The findings indicated that two of every three mothers with preschool children favored change and half of those desiring changes indicated preference for day care centers:

Desired alternative child care	Mothers of preschool-age children (percent)
No change desired	37
Change desired	64
to care in home	23
care in other's home	5
day care center	33
other	2

About three in ten mothers who were not in the work force indicated that they would prefer day care centers for their youngest child if they were to work. Over half of black mothers but not quite one-fourth of white mothers would have preferred this form of care. Centers were also a more popular choice among nonworking single heads of households.

The choice of arrangement actually made by working mothers reflects the available options, not preferences. Eighteen percent of District of Columbia mothers with children under three years old and 28 percent with three- to six-year-old children preferred a group center for surrogate care. However, centers were not available, and mothers away from home on a regular basis had to make other arrangements to take care of their children.[9] The demand for formal day care centers apparently exceeds current capacity. Preferences for centers among nonworking mothers suggest to some that more mothers would enter the labor market if such facilities were available at a reasonable cost.

Expressions of interest may, however, not be indicative of practice, and

apparent shortages may be illusory. If experiments with low-income populations are predictive of all mothers, federally supported universal day care
may not be taken advantage of, even if it is provided free of cost. About 700
slots in five day care centers and a number of licensed day care homes with
subsidies ranging from 35 to 100 percent of cost were made available to
selected families in Gary, Indiana, as part of a negative income tax experi-
ment. Eighty percent of the mothers in the experimental sample were either
employed, looking for work, or in a training program, and the balance had
access to subsidized care even if they were not in the labor force.

After 1.5 years, interim results showed that only 9 percent of the 700 eligible families used the subsidized services, and the utilization of subsidized
services by families involved in the work force or in training was lower than
for nonworking mothers. Poor recruitment or communication would not
explain the low utilization, since notices of the service were sent to the eligible parents.[10] Only six of the fifty families who were offered totally subsidized care took advantage of the child-care services. However, the sample
was small and there may have been other subsidized care available in the
community. But it seems that working mothers preferred to make their day
care choice on other bases than cost alone.

Other studies support the assumption that availability of free high quality
day care centers does not dictate the mother's choice of care. An
antipoverty manpower program that contracted with a day care center
found that few clients took advantage of the service because of distance
from home, dislike of group care, and lack of knowledge about the center.[11]

A survey of low-income mothers who worked outside their homes in Vermont reported that 51 percent of mothers did not use available day care
facilities or would not use them if they were available. Although each
respondent could submit multiple reasons for spurning day care facilities,
three-fourths stated preference for current arrangements. More mothers indicated preference of caring for their own children or stated that their
children would not like care in a center than mentioned excessive cost as a
barrier to use of day care centers.[12]

A GAO report on federally assisted child-care services in California and
Pennsylvania, which included participants in the Work Incentive Program
(WIN) and recipients of social services under Title IV-A of the Social Security Act, reiterated the preferences of working mothers for privately arranged child care rather than center care. Despite the fact that contracted
facilities were of high quality, in compliance with federal interagency day
care requirements, parents enrolled in the WIN program overwhelmingly
elected cash allowances and made their own child-care arrangements. Many
children who were enrolled in the centers under the social services program
had a nonworking parent, and the benefits that were derived from the

program were related to child enrichment rather than parent self-sufficiency.

The study also revealed that effective program costs skyrocketed because of low attendance, which averaged 72 percent in Pennsylvania and 68 percent in California centers, while nine private day care centers serving the children of working parents who paid fees experienced 92 percent attendance rates. Within contracted centers, the higher attendance rates were associated with higher percentages of working parents and low attendance with high percentages of nonworking mothers. Staff and facilities were maintained on the basis of contracted enrollment. A drop in enrollment and daily attendance raised the effective cost of the service. In one GAO example, the cost of day care on the basis of capacity utilization was $5.40 per day, or $1,350 per year. Actual enrollment and attendance rates pushed costs to $22.50 per day, or $5,625 per year.[13]

WOULD EXPANDED DAY CARE AFFECT LABOR FORCE PARTICIPATION?

The Westinghouse, Ruderman, and other surveys showing wide approval of day care centers may reflect opinions which are not identical with behavior of parents. Perhaps responses by women to surveys questioning whether they would work if day care were available should be viewed not as referendums on day care but as socially acceptable comments.[14] Other indicators suggest that the dearth of institutionalized day care alternatives does not strongly affect the labor force behavior of women.

The relationship between availability of day care facilities and mothers' participation in the work force has been a matter of considerable public discussion. A 1970 Current Population Survey provided some insights. The study indicated that only 2 percent of mothers under fifty-five years of age who were not in the labor force were willing to work but were prevented from doing so because of family responsibility or inability to arrange child care.[15] A 1966 Census Bureau study of all women over sixteen years old who were not in the labor force found that 9 percent were willing to hold a job and 3.7 percent did not look for a job because of inability to arrange child care or because of other family responsibilities.[16]

The Urban Employment Survey (USES) of six city poverty areas found that two-fifths of women who were not in the labor force between July 1968 through June 1969 but who wanted work were not job hunting because of family responsibilities. But two out of three citing "child-care problems" as the impediment to labor force participation indicated a preference for taking care of their own children. Of the remaining third, about half indicated either that they distrusted babysitters or that they had not tried to find one, with the balance indicating they could not find a babysitter at an acceptable price or at any price. Twenty percent of the 64,000 families in the sample indicated they would use day care centers if they were available.[17]

A 1967 survey of thirty- to forty-four-year-old women with at least one child under eighteen years old who were not in the labor force indicated that child-care arrangements would be necessary for 61 percent of blacks and 54 percent of whites in order to accept employment. But apparently many women would still not have sought work even if day care facilities were available, since 72 percent of white women and 54 percent of black women with children under six years old rejected the survey's hypothetical job offer outright.[18] It seems that a majority of women not in the work force were not seeking employment at that time.

Pay, job status, and other factors may have more effect on labor force participation than the availability of child care. About one-fourth of black women and one-fifth of white thirty- to forty-four-year-old women with at least one child indicated that they would accept employment if certain conditions were met. However, the establishment of satisfactory child-care arrangements as a precondition for employment was mentioned relatively infrequently compared to pay or the health of the respondent. Only 4 percent of black women and 2 percent of white women, out of the total nonworking population, made satisfactory child care a condition of accepting a hypothetical job offer.[19] Potentially, improvements in earnings and labor forces status will affect demand for child care.

DOES IT PAY THE EMPLOYER
TO PROVIDE CHILD CARE?

Few employers provide or subsidize child care. One generous estimate of industry-sponsored child care suggested that between 150 and 200 private employers provided day care arrangements for approximately 5,000 children.[20] The reason for limited development appears to be that industry cannot afford to provide them. Additionally, industry may not be willing to accept the concept of differential remuneration on the basis of child-care needs.

The contention that formal day care is a service that attracts women into the labor force and stabilizes their participation has been tested by employers who sponsored centers or recruited day care mothers to care for children of employees. Whatever benefits may have accrued to the children or their parents, the benefits to the employer have usually not justified the cost.[21]

The Office of Economic Opportunity set up a child development center for employees in March 1972. Twenty percent of eligible employees used the center. Costs ran between $250 and $300 per child per month—far above the amount parents were willing to pay. Parent fees were adjusted on the basis of family income and covered little more than one-fifth the actual costs. The center did not stimulate new employment, and other benefits to the employer were minimal. Impressionistic evidence indicated little difference between the job performances of workers whose children were enrolled and those whose children were not. In summary, OEO found the center too costly and turned it over to the parents after fifteen months.[22]

In response to expressed employee desires, the Chesapeake and Potomac Telephone Company set up a day care center, designed originally to serve low-income personnel, in their District of Columbia office, with the company subsidizing half the child-care fee. During the first two years, only half the center capacity was utilized. The availability of a subsidized center had little effect on the company's ability to recruit or retain workers or reduce absenteeism.[23]

The KLH experimental child-care center set up near the Cambridge, Massachusetts, plant for children of employees was much heralded when it was established. However, in less than five years, the company deemed it a failure after running huge deficits while charging $2,400 per child per year.[24]

Employers who have used less expensive approaches to the day care needs of employees have been more successful. The Illinois Bell Telephone Company has recruited and trained babysitters to provide services in the employees' homes. Advantages to parents include flexibility, tailoring to specific needs, service to wide geographic areas, elimination of transportation problems, and low cost to the parents. The employer generated good will without large capital investment or assuming the responsibility of child care.[25] But even this effort was given up. It may be surmised that as the economy weakened, industry did not have to offer as many incentives to retain workers.

For the most part, industry has shied away from undertaking child-care responsibility because of the high cost involved and the doubtful benefits.[26] Turnover of women employees is high (35 percent in 1969, compared to 18 percent by male employees in the same year), and it is partly related to child-care problems. But no empirical evidence exists to show that provision of day care reduces turnover, despite the intuitive appeal of such an argument.[27] Working conditions and pay are apparently more relevant to job attachment.

Firms which predominantly employ women, especially firms in which individual jobs are highly interrelated, are more economically sensitive to absenteeism, turnover, and recruiting problems related to child-care needs. Also, when unemployment is low and some industries experience manpower shortages, firms are likely to display a heightened interest in child care. It is not surprising, therefore, that traditional leaders in industrial day care are hospitals and garment firms. The latter employ large numbers of women at low wages in rather unpleasant jobs, and the former traditionally face man-power shortages. They are perhaps among the few industries in which it pays the employer to arrange child-care facilities.

CHILD-CARE
OPTIONS

Although the traditional picture of American family life which places the mother in the home with young children has never been fully representative of life styles, current trends suggest this picture represents practices of a passing era. Increasingly, mothers of preschool-age children are combining work careers with family responsibilities.

Mothers accept outside employment for diverse reasons. For some the earnings are essential; some follow careers regardless of income needs; some simply prefer outside employment. While many mothers work to help support their families, the extent of family dependence upon their earnings for necessities varies.

On the other hand, the growing number of mothers with young children who head households have the option of accepting employment or welfare. Disproportionate numbers have multiple labor force handicaps, including poor educational preparation, few salable skills, and overwhelming family responsibilities. Many are minority group women who must overcome racial discrimination in addition to other problems. Single mothers experience high unemployment or low earnings when they find jobs and may find welfare preferable to low pay. Single mothers obviously have a special need for child care and other services.

If past practices are clues to future trends, the bulk of child-care arrange-ments for children of working mothers at least until age three or four will remain informal, in the home, and low cost. Although the government has undertaken increased responsibilities for four- and five-year-old children, either through school or day care centers, the expansion of the day care centers has not been as rapid as some expected and they still account for less than 10 percent of all work-related arrangements. The expansion of day care centers faces a number of stumbling blocks, the greatest of which is cost. Working mothers earn relatively low salaries, and their ability or will-ingness to pay for "quality" care is limited. Unless center care is subsidized as public schools are, only custodial care is within the economic grasp of most consumers. And poor-quality center care is probably less desirable than other options.

The extent to which subsidized child-care facilities would change labor force participation is uncertain, but limited evidence suggests that most non-working women are at home by choice. A system of subsidized arrangements not associated with low incomes may change the child-care practices of working women. Returns to employers who have experimented with employer-run child-care centers have been too minimal to justify the costs. Less expensive approaches, such as arranging for babysitters, may be all many industries will be willing to provide. If day care is to expand, the government will have to undertake the responsibility for the activity as it did in the case of "free" universal public education.

CHAPTER FOUR / CHILD
CARE—WHO PAYS, HOW MUCH,
AND FOR WHAT?

Multiple mechanisms have been devised to defray the costs of child care. Parents pay for only part of the outlays. Federal, state, and local governments contribute direct payments to schools, day care centers, and other types of care and indirectly defray the child-care outlays of working parents by granting tax deductions.

Only ballpark estimates of total outlays are possible. Roughly estimated, child-care and educational expenditures for preschool-age children carried a price tag of about $5.7 billion in 1973 (chart 5). Parents paid about two-fifths of the total; state and local governments paid about a third, and federal sources contributed about one-fourth.

WORK-RELATED
CHILD CARE

Expenditures for care of preschool-age children of working mothers accounted for only about four of every ten dollars spent on the care and education of young children. An estimated $2.4 billion purchased child-care services for working mothers in 1973. Direct parental outlays averaged about $280 a year per working mother, or 60 percent of the total cost. This

CHART 5. Ballpark figures for child care and education expenditures children under six years old, 1973.

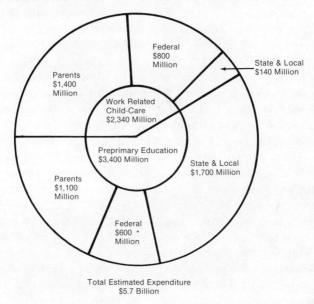

Total Estimated Expenditure
$5.7 Billion

Source: John R. Shea *et al., Years for Decision,* p. 13; and other sources.

figure disguises the fact that over half of all working mothers with preschoolers pay nothing for child care; some pay minimal cost, and some pay very high costs.

Federal-state child-care expenditures provide services for poor children under fifteen years old. About half of the children who are provided with care through federal programs are under six years old. However, since care of children under six is much costlier than for other children, it may be assumed that the bulk of government expenditures for child care was for preschool-age children.

Federal programs contributed about $800 million for work-related child care, close to a third of total child-care expenditures for 1973. More than $500 million was expended to induce mothers on welfare to train or find jobs, to provide income incentives permitting welfare recipients to keep a larger portion of their earnings, and to offer child care to other poor and near-poor mothers that would, it was hoped, remove work impediments.

In addition, federal income tax deductions for work-related child-care expenses cost the federal treasury an estimated $260 million in 1973. While the former provided care to less than a million children, predominantly those from poor or near-poor homes, the latter contributed to the care of several million children, most of whom lived in more affluent families.

State and local contributions for child care are primarily matching shares for federal welfare programs. States are required to pay 10 percent of child-care costs under the Work Incentive Program, 25 percent of outlays for social services, and anywhere from 18 to 50 percent of costs of the income disregard for AFDC mothers, depending on the state tax structure and per capita income. State contributions made up only about 5 to 10 percent of total child-care expenditures for work-related care.

Not considered are services provided by church and community organizations. There are no data on the value of their contributions, and they probably provide a small but significant fraction of expenditures. Nonetheless, for some parents these organizations absorb the major portion of child-care costs.

Overall ballpark figures suggest, therefore, that annual cost of work-related child care for preschool-age children was in excess of $400 per child a year. However, "average" child-care cost does not apply to any single group of children. More than eight out of ten working mothers did not qualify for any federal program except, perhaps, for limited indirect tax subsidies. Over half the children in these families were placed in "cost free" care provided by family members or friends. If all parents paid $15 a week for each child receiving outside care, parents' outlays would be about $4.4 billion instead of less than $2 billion. But within the existing broad range of child-care costs, the amount parents must pay is not necessarily related to their means to do so.

AVERAGE COST

The cost of care and who pays depends on the type of care arrangement and whether the parent qualifies for federal help. For instance, proprietary day care centers, which generally serve parents who do not qualify for government programs, cost more out of the parent's pocket but are a far less expensive form of care than that provided in most nonproprietary centers serving governmentally-assisted populations. A study that sampled a cross-section of day care centers found that revenues equaled $556 a year per full-time equivalent child in proprietary day care centers and $1,140 in nonproprietary centers,. Ninety-eight percent of the costs of proprietary centers were paid for by parent fees, whereas parents covered only 22 percent of costs in nonproprietary centers. Although no effort was made to impute costs of donated services and space, it is evident that the proprietary centers operate at much lower per capita costs.[1]

Another study of twenty "quality" day care centers found the average annual cost per enrolled child equaled $2,131 in 1970. Federal, state, and local contributions paid 70 percent of the costs, with the balance coming from parent fees, in-kind contributions, and other sources.[2] These centers were not typical, but represented an expensive program offering developmental services to carefully selected populations. Over half of the children were in single-parent households. The high levels of state and federal support indicate that the majority of clients were poor or near-poor and were entitled to supportive social services.

Staffing ratios and quality account for the bulk of cost differentials. Staff costs make up between 70 and 80 percent of total day care budgets. The "quality" centers studied by Abt Associates maintained staff to child ratios ranging from 1:2.2 to 1:6.5, with a median staff to child ratio of 1 to 3.4. The Westinghouse-Westat study reported median staff ratios at 1 to 12 in custodial centers, 1 to 11 in centers with educational components, and 1 to 4 in developmental centers. The Abt centers also included much higher ratios of trained teachers than found by the Westinghouse-Westat study, which reported that only 1 in 20 custodial centers, 4 in 10 educational centers, and 6 in 10 developmental centers had certified teachers on their staffs. In developmental centers, there was one certified teacher for every thirty-five children. Three-fourths of all day care workers had high school educations or less.

The Chicago Council of Community Services found that average day care center costs equaled $2,320 per child in 1971, based on 2,000 hours of care.[3] Proprietary centers averaged $1,300 cost per year, while nonprofit centers cost $3,240. Cooperative- and church-run centers averaged $1,840 and $2,100, respectively. The higher the cost of services, the smaller the percentage carried by fees and parent contributions. Parents' fees and direct grants paid 88 percent of proprietary programs costs, 78 percent of cooperative program costs, 20 percent of church-run costs, and 10 percent of nonprofit center costs.[4]

FEDERAL STANDARDS

The 1968 federal government requirements for day care centers and day care homes estimated that "minimum" quality care in a day care center—defined as the "level essential to maintaining the health and safety of the child"—cost $1,245 per year, or about $5.20 per day. "Acceptable" day care included "a basic program of developmental activities as well as providing minimum custodial care," and cost an estimated $1,862 per year, or about $7.60 per day. "Desirable care," which included the full range of general and specialized developmental activities, carried an estimated annual price tag of $2,320, or nearly $10 per day.[5] In 1974 dollars these figures would be: minimum—$1,772; acceptable—$2,650; and desirable—$3,302.

Federal day care requirements regulate the type of day care center or home which can be subsidized under federally aided welfare programs. High-cost centers tend to be those operated on a nonproprietary basis, and they serve a clientele of predominantly "disadvantaged" children. As noted in the Abt study, the annual cost of "quality" centers averaged $2,131 per child in 1970, of which the parents paid 9 percent.[6] Proprietary centers apparently provide the type of care parents are willing to buy, while nonproprietary centers provide the type of care the government is willing to procure.[7] The rate that parents are willing to pay for child care has remained far below what the government has proposed for minimum care standards.

While care provided by government-sponsored programs is generally more costly than that purchased by parents, there are wide variations in the quality and cost of care provided. Some children are cared for in elaborate developmental centers costing $2,000 to $3,000 annually per child, while others are placed in whatever care their parents can arrange—often low-cost babysitting arrangements. The average annual federal outlay per child under the social services program of $968 in 1973 concealed extreme differentials in state practices.[8] The average annual federal cost ranged from $70 in North Dakota to $3,470 in Nebraska. While some states have developed costly programs for disadvantaged children, others neglected such activities, which resulted in the following distribution:

Annual federal outlays per child	Number of states
Below $500	19
$500–$1,000	9
$1,001–2,000	20
$2,000 and over	4

Under the Work Incentive Program, $38 million of direct federal outlays purchased a total of 894,000 months of child care in 1973 at an average monthly cost of $42 per child ($47 counting the local share). A considerable range in costs was reported for both in-home and out-of-home care across states (map 1). The 1973 median monthly federal child-care support paid to states for in-home care was $30, ranging from $4.10 in Mississippi to $122 in Maine. The median monthly federal cost for out-of-home care was $48, with state averages ranging from $7 in Rhode Island to $111 in Ohio.

Larger percentages of children under six years old, higher percentages of out-of-home care and care by nonrelatives, and higher percentages of children cared for in day care centers are all associated with high-cost

MAP 1. Average monthly federal payment for WIN child care, fiscal 1973.

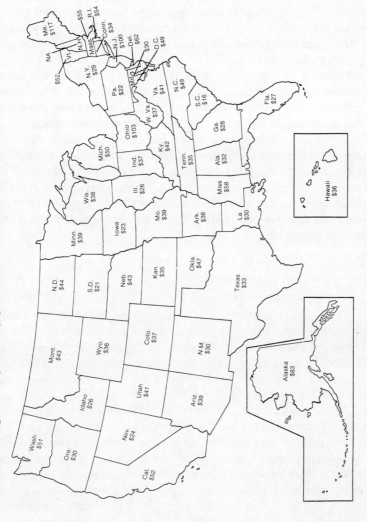

Source: U.S. Department of Health, Education, and Welfare, Community Services Administration. (unpublished tabulation).

Wash. $51
Ore. $30
Cal. $52
Nev. $24
Idaho $26
Mont. $43
Wyo. $36
Utah $41
Ariz. $39
N.M. $30
Colo. $37
N.D. $44
S.D. $21
Neb. $43
Kan. $35
Okla. $47
Texas $33
Minn. $39
Iowa $23
Mo. $39
Ark. $36
La. $30
Wis. $38
Ill. $26
Ind. $37
Ky. $42
Tenn. $35
Miss $58
Ala. $32
Mich. $50
Ohio $103
W. Va. $37
Va. $41
N.C. $49
S.C. $16
Ga. $28
Fla. $27
Pa. $22
N.Y. $29
Vt. $52
NA
Me. $117
N.H. $55
Mass. $54
R.I. $54
Conn. $34
N.J. $100
Del. $62
Md. $30
D.C. $49
Alaska $83
Hawaii $36

states.[9] But the effect of these variables upon the rate of reimbursement seems to depend on state policy more than on any other factor.

Total cost-of-care figures for children of working AFDC mothers must take into account costs of work expenses, which are disregarded in computing welfare payments. Gross estimates place the federal costs at $80 million, with states contributing an additional $50 million to care for about 175,000 children in 1973. This would place the average expenditure below that of other federal programs, perhaps reflecting choice of lower-cost care alternatives or care for older children.

The distribution of federal and state expenditures for child care is very uneven. Some children benefit from all types of services, while others receive minimum custodial care or no care at all. In some cases, low expenditures for child care disguise the fact that children attend compensatory education programs which are funded by the Office of Education, Model Cities, and other agencies. No doubt, there is some double counting of children who benefit from federally funded early childhood education and work-related child care. In many cases, the federal-state expenditures for work-related child care are low because the mothers prefer in-home arrangements with relatives or friends. There are other cases where only low-cost options are available.

QUALITY AND COSTS
OF CHILD CARE

A sample study of children cared for under federally funded programs in 1971 and 1972 compared the quality and costs of day care delivered in centers, in family day care homes, and in the children's own home by a caretaker.[10] Costs per child in day care centers equaled $2,110 annually, nearly double the cost of in-home care and more than triple the outlays in day care homes (chart 6).

It may be supposed that the less spent, the shoddier the product, but an analysis of facilities and services offered by the three types of day care indicated little correlation between cost and quality. Day care homes generally had more adequate indoor and outdoor space than centers, but centers generally had greater implementation of safety precautions. On balance, the quality of the care delivered was about equal under the three forms of care arrangements.

Children in day care centers received from 40 to 60 percent less care and teaching services than children in family day care homes and in-home settings, but staffs in centers were much more likely to be professionals and specialists in the field of child care and education. The survey did not attempt to pass judgment on whether the professional care was more produc-

CHART 6. Costs per child under alternative day care settings funded by federal programs, 1972.

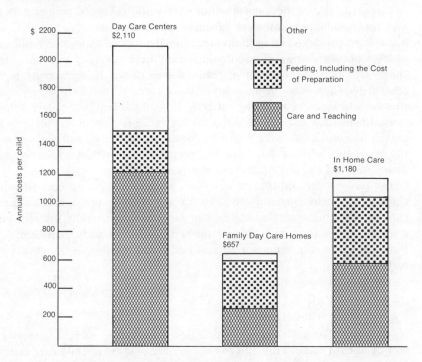

Source: AVCO Corporation, *A Demonstration Care Review System*, Final Report Contract HEW-SRS 71-48, "Cost of Day Care" (Washington: AVCO International Division, 1973), p. 10

tive or efficient than the home care. All sampled centers and almost all residential settings provided learning activities. However, centers were more likely to have formal, structured programs. Child care in homes was more likely to utilize educational television than was center care.[11]

Home-based caretakers were found to offer more individual attention, affection, gentleness, and sympathetic help and understanding to their charges than did staffs of center-based programs. On the other hand, day care centers were more likely to use reasoning and reinforcement than criticism or punishment for disciplining children. However, all caregivers' discipline methods tended to be "middle of the road," relying on no one discipline technique exclusively.[12]

Residential and center personnel were found to be equally mindful of detecting symptoms of illness, but centers were more likely to provide professional health care personnel and continued professional supervision. Over 90 percent of centers and about three-fourths of residential facilities had a first aid kit and one or more persons trained in administering first aid. While fewer residential facilities were directly linked to professional health care delivery mechanisms, they were better equipped than centers to care for sick children instead of having to send them home.

All types of day care facilities were found to serve children a sufficient number of meals, and the food intake for any week generally satisfied nutritional requirements. Residential facilities were found to serve more high-protein foods, whereas centers served more green vegetables. Centers were more apt to teach good eating patterns. In general, family day care homes ranked below the in-home facilities and day care centers in providing good nutrition. Food costs were generally higher in residential settings because the economies of bulk purchase and preparation were not available, and diets contained a higher percentage of expensive protein.

The study concluded that care in home settings is the most cost-effective child-care system currently purchased under federal programs. In-home care becomes more cost effective when capacity is more fully utilized. For instance, each caregiver could provide services for an additional child, effecting a substantial reduction in unit costs, without loss in the quality of care.

PARENTS' PAYMENTS
FOR CHILD CARE

The different methodologies used by the various surveys to cost child care make it difficult to estimate the relation of child-care expenditures to family income. Moreover, payment by parents does not reflect total costs of providing care, even where governments are not involved. Opportunity costs of relatives and friends offering "free" care are difficult to ascertain.

The 1970 Westinghouse-Westat survey included a disproportionate number of low-income households and focused, therefore, on subsidized facilities. Only 10 percent of all arrangements involved direct parental payment of $13 or more a week. In-home arrangements were substantially cost "free," reflecting care provided by family members (chart 7). Sixteen percent of low- and middle-income working mothers with preschool-age children and 51 percent with school-age children were not willing to pay anything for the most preferred form of day care.[13]

The Ohio University longitudinal studies, directed by Professor Herbert Parnes, documented variations in child-care costs incurred by black and white mothers. Cost-"free" arrangements, including self-care by fathers and siblings or care by mothers while working, were not covered in the study. In 1967, the median daily child-care cost to employed mothers thirty to forty-

CHART 7. Most low income working mothers arranged care for preschool children at minimal direct cost, 1968.

Total Working Mothers with
Child-Care Arrangements

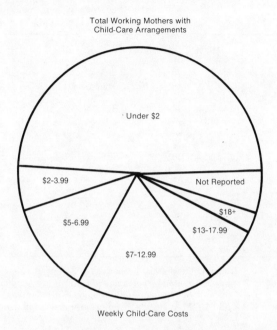

Weekly Child-Care Costs

Source: Westinghouse Learning Corporation and Westat Research, Inc., *Day Care Survey 1970—Summary Report and Basic Analysis* (Rockville, Md.. Westinghouse Learning Corporation and Westat Research, 1971), p. 187.

four years old was $2.75 for whites and $1.00 for blacks. In the following year, the costs for fourteen- to twenty-four-year-old employed mothers, most of whom had only preschool-age children, amounted to $2.85 per day for whites and $1.84 for blacks (table 6). The higher average costs to younger black mothers reflect the younger ages of their children, who require more care and greater use of formal facilities.

The Ohio Center data indicated that in-home care by nonrelatives was the most expensive option and the most frequent choice of child care by white women over thirty years old. The second most expensive option was care provided in the babysitter's home, and it was utilized most frequently by young white women. The rise of government, industry, and community subsidies to selected clienteles brought down the cost of day care centers to the families utilizing the facilities. Care by relatives remained the least expensive option. Nonetheless, costs exceeded $10 a week for one-fifth of the black families and almost two-fifths of white families who made such arrangements.

TABLE 6. Daily child-care costs of fourteen- to twenty-four-year-old mothers, 1968.

Arrangement	Total	No cost	$0–1.99	$2.00–2.99	$3.00–4.99	$5.00+	Median cost
All Whites	100%	16%	11%	27%	38%	9%	$2.85
In home							
relatives	18	45	4	29	23	—	2.04
nonrelatives	7	14	10	—	51	25	4.00
In caretaker's home							
relatives	28	24	14	31	26	6	2.32
nonrelatives	42	—	9	30	50	11	3.40
Group care center	5	—	30	14	40	16	3.15
All Blacks	100%	26%	28%	23%	21%	2%	$1.84
In home							
relative	26	61	21	10	8	—	no cost
nonrelative	7	—	37	9	38	16	3.20
In caretaker's home							
relatives	34	28	24	31	17	—	1.90
nonrelatives	23	3	39	26	30	3	2.35
Group care center	10	—	33	30	37	—	2.75

Source: John R. Shea, Roger D. Roderick, Frederick A. Zeller, Andrew I. Kohen and Associates, *Years for Decision: A Longitudinal Study of the Educational and Labor Market Experience of Young Women*, Vol. 1, (Columbus, Ohio. State University Center for Human Resources Research, 1971), p. 135, and mimeographed table from same.

The majority of child-care arrangements, especially informal arrangements with family members, involve little cost to parents. Low-income women depend on informal care to a much greater extent than middle-income women. Women with younger children pay more for child care. Six percent of young mothers paid upward of $5 a day in 1968 for day care, which amounted to $1,250 a year for full-time, full-year workers, a sum close to the federal cost estimate of minimum care in a center for three- to five-year-olds.

CHILD CARE AND WOMEN'S EARNINGS

The cost of preschoolers' day care services added to work expenses can easily absorb the total earnings of some women working full-time. In 1972, the median earnings of working wives was $3,183, and it was $5,925 for those who worked full time. Disregarding the costs of transportation and other work-connected expenses or the imputed costs of performing household tasks in addition to work (overtime duty), it is apparent that the daily salary of at least half of working women did not provide the cost of a single child's day care meeting federal standards.

TABLE 7. Daily cost of child-care arrangements and rate of pay for women fourteen to twenty-four years old who use child-care arrangements, 1968.

	Hourly wage rate		
Daily cost of child care	Less than $1.50	$1.50–$1.99	$2.00+
Whites			
No cost	18%	12%	14%
Less than $1.00	7	2	5
$1.00–$1.99	7	12	2
$2.00–$2.99	51	26	19
$3.00–$4.99	18	41	48
$5.00+	0	7	12
Median cost	$2.35	$2.92	$3.42
$\frac{\text{Median cost}}{\text{Median daily earnings}}$	21%	21%	17%
Blacks			
No cost	17%	33%	20%
Less than $1.00	6	0	0
$1.00–1$.99	54	16	15
$2.00–$2.99	24	27	14
$3.00–$4.99	0	22	45
$5.00+	0	2	5
Median cost	$1.50	$2.04	$3.04
$\frac{\text{Median cost}}{\text{Median daily earnings}}$	13%	15%	15%

Source: John R. Shea *et al.*, *Years For Decision*, p. 139.

Child-care expenditures which absorb half of net earnings may make labor force participation of mothers literally "slave labor." A professional woman working full time earned $8,744 in 1972. If her child-care bill was $2,600, her annual income after child-care outlays would drop to $6,144. The take-home pay would, of course, be much less after payroll and income tax deductions and adjustments for work-connected expenses were considered.

Willingness to pay for child care is related to earnings (table 7). Nevertheless, costs of day care are higher in a relative sense for low earning women, and young mothers pay more in relative and absolute terms because young children require more constant and costly care. Young white working mothers with preschool-age children spent about one-fifth of their earnings on child care, and black mothers spent about one-sixth. It is probable that blacks on the average pay less because their total family income is less.[14]

Clearly, day care expenditures consume a significant proportion of women's earnings. If all women were required to buy child-care services as prescribed by federal guidelines, the average income bite would come close to half of the mothers' earnings.

PREPRIMARY EDUCATION

School programs for children under six years old are not restricted to children of working mothers, but they do have great impact on family child-care needs and may also reduce child-care costs. In 1974, an estimated $3.4 billion was expended for kindergartens, nursery schools, and special compensatory programs. State and local tax dollars provided about half of this amount, primarily to support public kindergartens and nursery schools. Federal funds subsidizing the cost of compensatory programs for the disadvantaged accounted for less than a fifth of total outlays. Parents paid directly for about a third of the $3.4 billion estimated outlays in 1973 for nursery school and kindergarten programs.

Average per pupil costs are available for total school enrollment, but not by age or grade. The U.S. average elementary expenditure per pupil in the 1972–73 academic year equaled $1,026 and ranged from $1,584 in New York to $590 in Alabama.[15] The per pupil expenditure for kindergarten is less than that spent on primary schools because kindergartens are generally run on part-day sessions. In many schools, the same teachers and facilities accommodate two sessions, servicing twice the number of children as the primary grades. A larger percentage of kindergarten systems are located in northern and western states, which also have higher average per pupil expenditures than those in the South. Assuming that school systems which included public kindergartens averaged per pupil expenditures of $1,100 in 1972–73 and that the cost of part-day kindergarten was two-thirds that of full-day primary school (allowing for higher staffing ratios and additional transportation costs), average per pupil cost was about $740. This is an upper limit estimate for part-day programs, and the probable average cost of kindergarten may be below this level.

The requirements of nursery schools or play schools in a public system would probably be similar to those of kindergarten, but would perhaps require higher staffing ratios. Average per child costs on a half-day session may run about $800 per school year. The private expenditures for kindergartens and nursery schools probably are about the same as those for public schools. Again, private organizations and church groups contribute an undetermined portion of expenditures, but parents foot most of the bill.

Special compensatory programs are far more expensive than programs serving the general population but are restricted to a much smaller group and are paid for primarily with federal funds. Part-day, full-year Head Start programs run about $1,400 a year per child, with full-day services costing more. Federal outlays pay about 80 percent of this amount, with local sources paying the balance. Other federal funds for compensatory programs supplement services provided in local public schools. In 1973, some 700,000 poor children received compensatory preprimary education in federally funded programs. Nearly 300,000 attended Head Start projects, and the rest were enrolled in public schools offering special programs funded by the Elementary and Secondary Education Act. While the $400 million federal expenditures for Head Start played the major role in supporting social service programs for poor children, states and local sources contributed at least that much for the education of poor children in public school systems serving all children.

ARE COSTS DISTRIBUTED EQUALLY?

Checking the check stubs is far better than reading tea leaves in discerning individual desires and government policies. Expenditures for child care and education contain a number of important lessons.

First, a sizable portion of care and education expenditures comes from public coffers. Federal expenditures play a very important role, especially in delivering child-care and educational programs to children in poor families. Recognizing that the poor are least able to purchase such services, federal policy has defined the quality of the services that poor children need, and federal funds have paid most of the cost. But the distribution of services is uneven, partly reflecting state and local policies governing eligibility and partly reflecting insufficient resources.

Federal allocations suggest greatest concern for poor children, attempting to provide them compensatory education and to induce their parents to work and achieve self-support. Federal contributions, consequently, make up a small portion of direct expenditures for the care and education of children in more affluent families, but taxation policy may expand subsidies to mothers who already work by liberalizing eligibility and deductions for child-care expenditures. Following traditional policies, state and local expenditures have provided kindergartens and nursery schools to the general population, leaving special concern for poor children largely in the federal domain.

Second, while parents pay most child-care costs, direct outlays tend to be low. Some mothers want better care but cannot afford to pay. Many do not have to pay for child-care services provided by relatives or friends, or obtained through subsidized programs. Some mothers have no choice but to pay more than they want to, but most will choose the least expensive option as long as they are satisfied with the care. If higher quality and more expensive services were paid for by public funds, undoubtedly more mothers would use them. Other things being equal, free services are more attractive than those that require payment. Convenience and such intangibles as outlook and philosophy of parents and caregivers also affect demand for such services.

Out-of-pocket outlays of parents suggest considerable interest in early education for three- and four-year-olds, while public outlays pay for most five-year-olds in kindergarten programs. Perhaps the choice of low-cost informal child-care arrangements reflects that in some cases these arrangements supplement children's participation in education programs which are in part financed by public sources and in part paid for by parents.

Third, federal standards for adequate and desirable child-care programs and the high price tags they carry suggest a goal that is out of reach of most parents. The standards are quite arbitrary. In fact, while some low-cost arrangements leave much to be desired, most are satisfactory. Children are provided essential needs and more, but since these services are largely donated, total costs are low.

Finally, differences in child-care expenditures suggest considerable inequities. Some communities provide free public education for preschoolers; in others, parents have to pay or go without. Some poor working mothers get extensive help, while others, who may live in another state or have only slightly higher family incomes, must pay the full cost of child-care services. Direct provision of high-cost services through government programs adds to the large variation in services children get. Since resources are not sufficient to serve every child, many are excluded.

CHAPTER FIVE / BEYOND
MERE CARE

In the previous chapters, child care has been viewed as a service to mothers who work. Under the best of conditions, help for mothers also contributes to the children's development. Much of institutional care provided for children less than six years old, however, has as its main purpose the provision of education, and programs must be evaluated in this context. For the most part, the extent to which preprimary education programs meet employment-related needs is incidental. But some have argued that society should expand the scope of education programs to meet child-care needs of families.

During its first century, the American society reached a consensus on the desirability of providing education to all children and, indeed, determined to make it compulsory. But the age at which children should embark on their formal educational careers has not been settled during the second century of the republic. At what age does it become more beneficial for children to enroll in an institutional setting than to remain under the exclusive supervision of their mothers? Are children better off if they receive elaborate child-care and educational services rather than mere custodial care? All child-care and educational programs contain some "babysitting," and none are totally devoid of learning experiences for children. However, there is considerable argument over what combination of services is most beneficial for the child and, indeed, what the educational program prior to age six years should be.

The benefits of early education and the best means of caring for preschool children remain unsettled. It is impossible to demonstrate to the satisfaction of all concerned the relative payoffs of early institutional education versus the benefits of mothers staying at home to care for children. There are any number of personal and professional preferences regarding child rearing, largely reflecting personal and social values rather than scientific judgments. It is, however, a fact that more and more young children are being cared for outside the home, and more of this care is being combined with educational services designed to cater to their well-being and to serve as prep schools to embarking on years of compulsory education.

THE INFANCY OF INFANT SCHOOL

Interest in establishing institutions to provide for the care and education of young children of working women dates back to the industrial revolution. These early social experiments established lofty goals. They promised not only to fill the educational and care roles formerly provided by mothers but also to improve the poverty-ridden environment of the laboring class and to help build upright characters in the children of the poor.

Friedrich Froebel, a nineteenth-century German, was the father of kindergarten. He not only developed a comprehensive theory of early childhood education but also contributed a detailed model for it, which included specific games, play, and storytelling as vehicles for realization of the child's latent potential. Working with retarded and poor children, Maria Montessori, another major pioneer in preschool education, founded in 1907 the *Casi dei Bambini* (the children's house) in Rome. Believing that children learn concepts through sensory perception and experiences, she devised games, puzzles, geometric forms, colors, and other didactic equipment designed to help children learn at their own pace in an atmosphere of freedom.

The first American kindergarten for English-speaking children was founded by Elizabeth Peabody in 1860.[1] Seventeen years later, St. Louis hosted the first American public kindergarten. Since then, kindergartens have experienced continued growth in the United States. These institutions have caught on both as positive educational and social experiences for young children and as vehicles for the Americanization of immigrant children.[2] Normally attached to the existing public school systems, kindergartens provided half-day classes for four- and five-year-old children. The 1929 White House Conference on Child Health and Protection deemed the future of kindergartens assured. It recognized kindergarten's primary purpose as "education rather than relief" and acknowledged its value as part of the public school system.[3]

The American nursery school aimed at three- and four-year-olds developed along different lines. A number of university education and psychology departments founded nursery schools as built-in laboratories to observe early childhood behavior. Other schools were established to train young women for teaching and for motherhood. A uniquely American variation of the nursery school was the cooperative venture run by parents, the first of which was established in 1916 by University of Chicago faculty wives and alumni. But there was less acceptance for separating children and parents at such a tender age, and nursery schools were slow to expand. During the 1930s, nursery schools received some federal support under the Works Progress Administration to employ teachers and help impoverished children. The World War II Lanham Act funded nursery schools and day care centers for children of women working in war-related industries. But these measures were short-lived.

Most American nursery schools developed under private auspices and served middle- and upper-income families. However, since 1965, Head Start and other federal programs have brought nursery school services to increasing numbers of poor children. From the very beginning, the emphasis in American nursery schools has been on education. This contrasts sharply with the "day nursery," the predecessor of day care centers, which provided protective custody for infants and young children of poor working mothers. Sponsors included social agencies and philanthropic organizations and were located mostly in large urban areas.

Although kindergartens, nursery schools, and day care centers share common ancestral heritages, they developed along divergent paths. The educational goals of kindergartens and nursery schools exempted them from criticisms directed at day care centers. Broad public support of kindergartens led to their adoption by a majority of the public school systems. Nursery schools developed largely under private auspices and provided services to middle-income families who could afford to pay. More recently, an increasing number of communities are accepting nursery schools as a public function.

THE "KIDDIE" COLLEGE
EXPANSION

During the 1960s, the American educational system expanded services down the age spectrum to reach increasing percentages of three- to five-year-old children (table 8). The number of three- to five-year-olds in the population declined from 12.5 million in 1964 to 10.3 million in 1973. During that decade, preprimary-school enrollments increased from 25.5 percent of the population to 41 percent. The greatest proportional increases in enrollment were among the youngest children. In 1964, only 4.3 percent of

TABLE 8. Since 1964 the percentage of scholarly toddlers has increased significantly.

Age and race	Total population (in thousands)		Percent enrolled in schools	
	1964	1973	1964	1973
TOTAL	12,496	10,344	25.5	40.9
3-year-olds				
white	3,383	2,977	4.2	14.0
nonwhite	655	579	4.4	16.9
4-year-olds				
white	3,522	2,903	14.5	32.6
nonwhite	626	540	16.8	42.6
5-year-olds[1]				
white	3,503	2,817	59.2	76.6
nonwhite	607	527	50.4	73.1

[1] About 10 percent of 5-year-olds were enrolled in elementary schools in 1973, pushing total enrollments to 87 percent for white 5-year-olds and 82 percent for nonwhites.
Source: Gordon E. Hurd, *Preprimary Enrollment Trends of Children Under Six: 1964–1968* (Washington: Government Printing Office, 1970), pp. 26–28; and U.S. Bureau of the Census, "Nursery School and Kindergarten Enrollment: October 1973," Series P-20, No. 268, August 1974, Table 1.

all three-year-olds and 14.9 percent of four-year-olds were enrolled in schools.[4] By 1973, the percentages enrolled had jumped to 14.5 and 34.2 percent.

The clamor for institutionalized ABCs and early social interaction was reinforced by several trends. The increasing number of infant scholars resulted from new federal funding of early education projects, the increased number of working mothers with small children, the increased interest and support by state and local school boards of public kindergartens and nursery schools, and the declining numbers of six-year-old children entering schools each year, which freed capacity for younger enrollees.

A total of 4.2 million children attended nursery schools and kindergarten in 1973. According to one authoritative projection, by the end of the 1970s, 55 percent of three-year-old children, 77 percent of four-year-olds, and virtually all five-year-olds will attend school.[5] These estimates rest on the assumption that the taxpayer will be willing to pay the cost of the mounting preprimary education.

Public schools have assumed an expanded role in preprimary school. Altogether, 2.9 million children attended kindergarten in 1973, and the proportion of five-year-olds enrolled in kindergarten jumped from 57 percent in 1964 to 74 percent in 1973. The public kindergarten system served 2.1 million five-year-olds and 0.3 million four-year-olds in 1973, or nearly nine of every ten kindergarten scholars enrolled in public facilities.

TABLE 9. Although proportionately fewer nonmetropolitan three- to five-year-olds attend school, they are more likely to be enrolled in public facilities, 1973.

	Central Cities	Suburban	Nonmetropolitan
Total population (in thousands)	3,080	3,998	3,265
Enrolled in school	44%	44%	34%
Enrolled in public schools	30	26	26
Ratio of public enrollments to total	69	60	75

Source: Derived from U.S. Bureau of the Census, "Nursery School and Kindergarten Enrollment: October 1973," Series P-20, No. 268, August 1974, Tables 3 and 7.

Nursery schools remain largely a private undertaking, although the public schools are expanding to the lower age bracket. Between 1964 and 1973, nursery school enrollment jumped from 471,000 to 1.3 million. The enrollment in publicly supported schools nearly quintupled, from 81,000 to 394,000, while enrollment in the private schools rose by 143 percent. But in 1973, private facilities still accounted for 70 percent of 1.3 million children enrolled in nursery schools.

Preprimary-school enrollment is related to race, residence, family income, and the occupation and education of parents. In the past, central cities provided more public facilities and, consequently, led the nation in the percentage of children in preprimary schools. In 1973, four of every ten city nursery school enrollments were in publicly supported systems, compared with one-fifth of suburban enrollments and two-fifths of enrollments in nonmetropolitan areas. Both central cities and suburban areas outpace nonmetropolitan areas in the proportion of three- to five-year-olds enrolled in school; but nonmetropolitan children are most likely to attend public schools, while suburbanites are most likely to purchase private facilities (table 9).

The South also lagged behind in establishing public systems and had the lowest percentage of five-year-olds enrolled in kindergartens—59 percent compared to 79 percent or more in other regions in 1972. Of children who did attend kindergarten, over one-third were enrolled in private facilities, compared to less than 10 percent in other regions. The South accounted for over three-fifths of all American children in private kindergartens.[6]

Educational efforts in the South have been hampered by historically lower per capita incomes and high demands for services. In the 1969–70 school year, all southern states except Virginia, Florida, and Texas spent more than the national average of 7 percent of per capita income on education, yet all spent less than the average per capita amount for education.[7] Recent federal contributions for elementary and secondary education have disproportionately benefited the South and will perhaps allow the region's public school system to catch up with the rest of the nation in the provision of public kindergartens.

Since data became available in 1964, a larger percentage of black than white three- and four-year-olds have attended nursery school. This reflects not only the tradition of using preschool as an alternative to child care but also the push of Great Society programs to provide compensatory programs, especially for young disadvantaged children before they reach the first grade. Traditionally, a larger percentage of white five-year-old children attended kindergarten; however, that disparity has been closing with the extension of the public kindergarten system.

In white families, the higher the family income, the more likely the children are to attend nursery school. However, in black families the correlation between income and enrollment pattern is not so clearly defined. What apparently happens is that more affluent white families purchase services, but facilities have been made available in ghetto areas giving black children access. Black preprimary children are far more likely to attend public systems (chart 8).

Higher percentages of nursery school students and black children were enrolled in full-day sessions in 1973:[8]

| | Percent of enrolled children in full-day programs | | |
	Total	White	Black
3-year-olds	35	30	58
4-year-olds	26	19	53
5-year-olds	19	16	37

Full-day programs are more common in poverty areas and may double as child-care centers for working mothers.

A number of factors have contributed to the rise of preprimary enrollment; these include increased availability of services, greater affluence, and fewer children per family. Contrary to widespread notions, the rising work experience of women was not necessarily the most important factor. Increased federal support of preprimary schools favors the poor, frequently without consideration of the mothers' work status. Head Start alone increased nursery school enrollment by 270,000 between 1965 and 1973. Ninety percent of these children were poor.

The Elementary and Secondary School Act supported the addition of preprimary facilities to public systems which formerly had no kindergartens or nursery schools. In 1973, federal funds subsidized nursery school facilities for 174,000 children and kindergartens for 273,000 children. Other

CHART 8. Proportionately more black children than whites enrolled in public nursery schools and kindergartens, 1973.

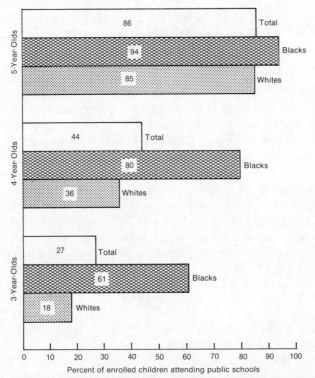

Source: U.S. Bureau of the Census, "Nursery School and Kindergarten Enrollment: October 1973," Series P-20, No. 268, August 1974, Table 1.

funds were used to augment ongoing programs with additional personnel and special services. These grants, though thinly spread, were awarded to school districts with high concentrations of children who were educationally disadvantaged by reason of poverty, cultural or linguistic isolation, or other handicaps. Aside from directly augmenting resources for preprimary schools, Elementary and Secondary School Act programs probably stimulated interest in expanding public systems in areas not receiving assistance.

The expansion of the school system down the age spectrum may be partially an accommodation to the declining number of school-age children as well as a response to federal programs. After having peaked in 1957, the number of births in the United States declined from 4.3 million in 1961 to 3.1 million in 1973:[9]

Year	Thousands of births	Year	Thousands of births
1961	4,268	1968	3,502
1962	4,167	1969	3,571
1963	4,098	1970	3,718
1964	4,027	1971	3,556
1965	3,760	1972	3,256
1966	3,606	1973	3,141
1967	3,521		

Enrollments in kindergarten through eighth grade peaked in the 1969–70 school year at 33.2 million children and declined by almost 800,000 children in the following three years.[10] The recent decline in the number of births suggests elementary school enrollment will continue to decline. Excess capacity plus an oversupply of teachers has apparently stimulated public schools to provide services to preschool children. Expansion of public schools to serve adults seeking continuing post-secondary education is foreclosed by, or might involve a clash with, the expanding junior and community college interests. Pressure on school systems to contract or fill unused capacity with younger students will expand in the future because fewer children are being born. The 3.5 million children reaching age six in 1974 will decline by 12 percent in 1979.

EARLY EDUCATION IN
OTHER COUNTRIES

The rapid expansion of schools for three-, four-, and five-year-olds in the United States has been paralleled in many Western European nations and in Canada.[11] In Belgium, enrollment in schools is almost universal starting at age three; in France and the Netherlands, over three-fourths of children begin school by age four; in Canada and Italy, over 80 percent of children start school at age five; in Sweden, the effective age of school entry is six years.

The heightened interest in preschool education in Europe as well as in the United States can be traced to governmental desires to expand and democratize educational opportunities, to the belief that early education benefits the child, to the decline in family size, and to the greater participation of mothers in the labor force. However, preliminary findings based on the experience of European countries suggest that effective age of school entry does not insure improved academic achievement as children mature. In countries where children enter school at a younger age there seems to be a slightly beneficial impact on achievement in mathematics but a slightly negative impact on reading achievement.[12] The experiences of other countries offer no more conclusive support to arguments of academic benefits from early education than experiences in the United States.

DAY CARE CENTERS AND THE
EDUCATIONAL ESTABLISHMENT

One additional movement has attempted to blend educational goals with traditional "welfare" services. The nursery school establishment has long belabored the distinction between its institutions and "day care" centers, contrasting the educational and social goals of nursery schools with the "custodial" services of day care centers. In the past, day care centers often provided protective care for children who, according to the judgment of social workers, did not receive adequate care from their parents. As more mothers who suffered from neither marital disruption nor financial distress have entered the work force, day care centers have become identified as desirable institutional arrangements for the care of children. Proprietary and community-run centers have developed to fill the demand, but most private purchasers cannot afford the cost of care provided through federal programs for poor children. Consequently, the day care center system fosters economic and social homogeneity of clientele, segregating the poor who qualify for free services but excluding most of the children whose families cannot afford to pay for the expensive care required by federal standards.

Early day care facilities were largely custodial—they were safe harbors. Many present programs, especially those aided by public funds, deemed that children had to be given opportunities to learn and grow, and that mere custodial care would not do. Day care programs serving various populations added educational components, and some programs concentrating on the needs of the poor added health care, parent counseling, and other services. Some day care centers have moved closer to the nursery school model, while others continue to provide traditional custodial services.

Expansion of Day Care Centers—Real or Illusory? The upgrading was to some extent the result of federal quality standards. All day care services provided directly or purchased with federal funds must meet the federal day care requirements issued in 1968. These regulations specify a licensing procedure, staffing ratios, training requirements, environmental facilities, social, health, and nutrition services, and parent participation. The requirements should more properly be viewed as goals, since few child-care centers live up to the federal specifications.

Although most states require licensing of day care facilities, standards vary, and state enforcement budgets generally enable only cursory examination for physical safety and sanitation. About 90 percent of day care centers are licensed, but only about 10 percent of day care homes. Federal staffing requirements in day care centers generally exceed actual practice in most facilities. Groups of three-year-old children must be limited to fifteen or less and staffed with one adult for every five children; four- and five-year-old children are limited to twenty children per group with a minimum staffing ratio of one adult for every seven children. In addition, in-service training must be provided and nonprofessional staff must be given opportunities for advancement. These requirements compare with a 1969 industry average of a twelve to one child-staff ratio in full-day custodial centers and six to one in educational centers.[13]

Federal regulations required that facilities be safe and sanitary, and that they provide adequate indoor and outdoor space for free play, arrangements for naps, and isolation space for sick children. Educational opportunities and materials were to be provided for every child. In addition to social services, the centers were also required to provide dental and medical evaluation upon enrollment, and the children were to be fed nutritious meals. A center that cared for forty or more children was to select a parent advisory committee to permit parent participation in policy formulation.[14]

Few centers could live up to these stringent and costly center standards, and in recognition of reality, HEW officials have attempted to revise the federal day care requirements, setting a level more in keeping with actual practices. But formal revision of regulations never materialized, perhaps to avoid criticism that the proposed regulations signaled an abandonment of federal commitment to poor children.

The 18,400 licensed day care centers had a 1971 capacity to accommodate 719,000 children. An additional 60,000 slots were available in unlicensed arrangements. Day care centers must have been one of the fastest growing industries in America. During the eleven years prior to 1971, the number of centers in operation and their capacity had grown more than fourfold. The growth was shared by public, private nonprofit, and proprietary centers, and it was divided as follows in 1971:[15]

Total	Public	Private nonprofit	Proprietary
Centers 18,435[a]	8%	37%	49%
Capacity 719,000[a]	9	40	46

[a] Sum of percentages less than 100 because Tennessee and New Jersey did not report auspices.

Undoubtedly, some of the apparent growth was illusory and reflected recorded expansion, since state licensing boards certified formerly unlicensed centers in order to be eligible to receive federal subsidies.[16] However, the majority of centers were new facilities. According to 1970 findings, only half of the centers had been in operation for more than five years.[17]

Scope of Services. Although the services offered in day care centers vary from custodial to developmental, some basic activities are common to all. All centers provide children a structured environment supervised by adults outside the child's immediate family. In addition to basic care, centers may provide medical, dental, nutritional, and educational services. Social services for the family, parental education, and psychological services may also be offered in connection with day care services.

The "developmental" services are costly and are usually purchased only through government subsidized programs aimed at the poor. Consequently, "developmental" centers tend to serve a homogeneous group—poor children who tend to be children of one race. Although the report of the National Council of Jewish Women may not have been based on a totally representative sample, its findings indicated that day care centers were racially segregated due to the selection process.[18] Federally and philanthropically supported centers serve predominantly black clienteles, while proprietary centers serve predominantly white clienteles. More than 75 percent of 1970 enrollees in two of every three Head Start programs were black children, whereas three of every four children enrolled in 74 percent of the proprietary centers were white. What is implicit is that these systems also tend to segregate by economic class, with nonprofit centers enrolling those who cannot afford to pay and proprietary centers accepting those who can.

Some day care centers experience unutilized capacity while others have long waiting lists. This incongruity results from mislocation, pricing policies, or quality of services offered. Precise estimates of the number waiting for admission to day centers are hard to come by because the same children may be on several waiting lists. Barring duplication and unutilized slots, 55,000 children were on the 1970 waiting list for licensed facilities, requiring 12 percent expansion of total day care facility slots in order to accommodate them.[19] This amounted to about 1.3 percent of all preschool-age children of working mothers who were not cared for in a licensed day care center or home. The shortage might have been larger if "free" centers were available.

Wide differences exist in the quality of services provided by day care centers, as do corresponding variations in the cost. Benchmarks for quality include measurable practices such as low adult-child ratios, professional certification of teachers, adequate space, and physical and recreational facilities. Intangible negative factors such as oppressive atmosphere, regimentation, and overly strict discipline are also considerations. A 1972 study found proprietary centers the worst offenders in providing poor quality care.[20] Nonprofit centers provided generally better care at a lower charge to the enrollees, primarily because government and social agencies paid the bulk of the cost.

For very practical reasons, few centers meet the stringent federal standards. A sample low-cost budget adhering to federal interagency day care requirements estimated in 1971 an annual cost of $2,600 per three- to five-year-old child in full-day care. The annual cost per child in a high budget center was estimated at $3,700.[21] Even if the dollars were available, adequate supplies of facilities and properly trained manpower are lacking.

Federal yardsticks can measure "quality" only in terms of available resources, trained teachers, safe facilities, and other quantifiable benchmarks. The assumption or hope is that these criteria assure a desirable and warm environment for children.

Federal day care policies have stressed the needs of disadvantaged children, including migrant and mentally retarded children and children of poor working mothers and welfare mothers. "Quality" day care services that meet federal standards and combine educational and developmental services with child care are available to some AFDC children and to a variety of smaller manpower and child welfare program children. Relatively little attention has been paid to the needs of other working mothers and their children.

Some slots in federally sponsored developmental centers are available to children whose parents do not work. The Westinghouse-Westat survey reported that the proportion of children with working mothers was 97 percent in custodial centers and 91 percent in centers with educational components, but only 83 percent in centers which offered developmental services.[22] Parents who are qualified for subsidized care occasionally succeed in placing their children in federally financed developmental day care programs even if the mothers do not work. When programs are designed to intervene on behalf of disadvantaged children to help them overcome handicaps, it is difficult to justify denying a child opportunity because of the mother's labor force participation.

COMBINING OVERLAPPING
SYSTEMS

As subsidized day care center facilities expand, the extent to which the functions of day care centers and preprimary-school systems overlap is becoming an increasingly pressing policy issue. Is the development of both systems desirable?

The day care center is restricted by most state licensing laws to a clientele three years old and over. Day care center services for children over six years old are available in few centers. As schools provide supervision for the large portion of the day, parents find the added center services less desirable. Primarily, day care centers serve three- to six-year-old children, with day care homes serving younger children. The majority of day care centers operate between ten and twelve hours per day—opening by 7:45 A.M. and closing at 6:00 P.M.[23] In comparison, kindergarten and nursery school schedules are usually contained within the school schedule and may be divided into morning and/or afternoon sessions.

Day care centers, nursery schools, and kindergartens serve the same age groups. Each provides opportunities for group play and experience with adult authority figures other than parents. The functions of day care centers and preschools differ in that the former provide a safe surrogate care first and may add developmental or educational features; the schools serve primarily an "educational" purpose, even though the impact of kindergarten or other preschool experience on later school achievement has been questioned.[24]

PAYOFFS FOR PRESCHOOL EDUCATION

The relative emphasis given to custodial care versus education within kindergartens, nursery schools, and day care centers is not clearcut; there is some of each in all three. The issue is, how much education and other services should be provided? An informed response requires knowledge about the payoffs of early childhood education and what works.

Many studies have been directed at assessing developmental deficiencies, isolating their causes, and constructing strategies for overcoming handicaps which later result in poor educational and labor force performance. The widely discussed Coleman Report of the preceding decade found that with the exception of Oriental-American children, minority children averaged lower scores on achievement tests than white children upon entry to the first grade, and that the gap in achievement widened by the twelfth grade. Furthermore, less controllable variables such as family background and classroom peer groups were found to be more important in determining achievement than early classroom exposure, teacher competency, or expenditures for education.[25]

While measures differ, poor children, who are disproportionately minority children, invariably do not perform as well as middle-class white children on standardized achievement tests, and these children are less successful in school.[26] Three streams of thinking, or, more appropriately dubbed, battle lines, have arisen to explain this phenomenon. To generalize, inferior IQ tests and school performance have been attributed to genetic, environmental, or measurement factors, or some combination of these factors.

The Genetic School—"Nature Is More Powerful than Education". Genetic pathology, a theory associating genetic performance with inherent inferior capability, usually considered the stock in trade of bigots, has recently been accorded respectability in some quarters. Arthur Jensen has argued that there are inherited differences in the abilities of black and white children, equaling about one standard deviation in favor of whites. The controversial Jensen study cited average IQ differences of fifteen points between white and black populations. When gross socioeconomic differences were controlled, the average gap declined, but only to eleven points.[27] Jensen found that black children tended to have higher associative learning skills than white children of the same IQ level and therefore appeared brighter than IQ scores predicted. Poorer performance occurred mainly in abstract analytical and conceptual measures. Jensen concluded that extreme environmental deprivation could prevent a child from reaching his potential but that an enriched environment could not push him past his natural abilities. He recognized that severe neonatal and prenatal deficiencies could cause permanent damage but contended that conditions of subsistence survival among pregnant women, new mothers, and families in general are largely absent in America. The implications of this thesis are that society must adjust the teaching demands, job criteria, and other societal hurdles to a standard that will allow all segments to share society's benefits.

The Environmental Pathology School—"As the Twig Is Bent the Tree's Inclined". The environmental pathology school attributes inferior performance of poor and minority children to (1) primary environmental pathology in the home, and (2) secondary environmental pathology in schools, which reject and even persecute children on the grounds that they lack middle-class attributes. According to this thesis, children are trapped in the "cycle of poverty" and denied achievement by middle-class standards because their families do not and cannot provide them with adequate mental tools, physical care, and nutritional needs to perform in school; thus schools tend to reinforce initial failures caused by inadequate home environments.

Primary environmental pathology theories were developed from studies of children who had lived in extremely deficient environments and whose apparent mental retardation was reversed after being placed in a rich environment. Among the most noted is Harold Skeels's study of retarded three-year-old orphanage wards during the 1930s. Children in the control group, which initially had a higher mean IQ, remained in a deficient orphanage environment, while the experimental group was placed in a state hospital for the mentally retarded where they received preferential treatment and attention. The control group children regressed in development while the experimental children climbed into the normal range and were subsequently adopted. Thirteen experimental children grew into self-supporting adults and completed a median of twelve years of schooling. Of the eleven surviving members of the control group (one died in an institution during adolescence), four remained institutionalized in adulthood, and the group completed a median of three years of school.[28]

➤ The notion that the human mind becomes less malleable with advancing age suggested that poor IQ scores and school performance were linked with inferior early environment. According to one study, socioeconomic levels significantly affect maternal teaching styles. The authors implied that learning problems of low socioeconomic group children were linked to inferior maternal teaching styles.[29]

Other studies have noted that as the result of home environment, poor children often begin formal education with limited vocabularies, poor articulation, and faulty syntax. Contending that lack of abstract conceptualization in language in lower-class homes poorly equips children with the conceptual tools needed for school, researchers have recommended such measures as developmental day care centers and special programs to improve language skills.[30]

The pathology of home environment thesis argues that numerous phenomena associated with poverty may affect the learning capabilities of children before they reach compulsory school age. These include lack of order in the home and lack of adequate nutrition caused by poor eating habits, not to mention lack of money and lack of medical care or the sophistication to spot and treat perceptual difficulties such as hearing or vision problems.

The secondary environmental pathology thesis holds that negative reactions on the part of schools and other social institutions cause children raised in poverty to think of themselves as failures and to act accordingly. For instance, one account of a ghetto school observed that as early as kindergarten, teachers grouped children according to such attributes as cleanliness of clothes, lightness of skin, and education level and marital stability of parents, and they singled out those with the highest socioeconomic backgrounds as the faster learners. The "fast learners" were seated closest to the teacher and received most of her attention, while the "nonachievers" were placed farthest from the teacher and ignored, and their failure to learn "rationalized" as innate inferiority.[31]

A different twist of the same theme is the teacher's belief that children cannot achieve because of inferior home environments. Children are not expected to achieve; therefore, they do not achieve, and their failure is attributed to pupil inadequacy rather than teacher failure or failure to teach.[32] A study by Rosenthal and Jacobson corroborated the thesis that children's performance adjusts to teacher expectations. But other experiments have been unable to replicate this study, suggesting that the original findings may have resulted from Hawthorne or placebo effects, experimental bias, or statistical errors. Aside from anecdotal interpretations, replicable studies which support the idea that students learn according to teacher expectations are lacking.[33]

The Measurement Pathology School—"You Can't Fit Square Pegs in Round Holes". The third interpretation of the reason poor and minority children fail to achieve on a par with middle-class white children argues that the culture gap implied in the environmental pathology idea is a matter of perspective and that black and other minority groups' dialects and cultures are *different,* not *deficient.* Children do not achieve as well on achievement tests because the tests are culturally and linguistically biased.[34]

A corollary point is the contention that schools refuse to reward black cultural behavior. Linguist Susan Houston has contended that the language heard by most researchers and school teachers is different and less rich than the language used in the homes of black children. The assumption that black dialect is an inadequate base for abstract thinking is challenged on the grounds that it is impossible to extrapolate cognitive patterns from language patterns and that, presumably, one could not speak at all if unaware of generalization and categorization. This does not deny the desirability of teaching standard English, because black dialect is widely considered substandard and may present a drag on upward mobility.[35]

The claim that black children do poorly on IQ tests because the testing environment and language is middle-class and therefore foreign has been disputed in a study of 100 black three- and four-year-old Head Starters. There were no significant differences in test scores whether the examiners, who were also black, used standard or dialect English, or used praise or candy as incentives for the children to perform well.[36] Another study compared the scores on tests using abstract reasoning with scores of more culturally biased subjects demanding greater language skills. Results indicated that blacks performed better on culturally biased tests.[37] One may question, however, whether the criteria on which IQ scores or class rank are awarded have any valid relationship to one's ability to hold a job and conduct adult affairs adequately.

DOES TUTORING TODDLERS
HELP?

The social implications of school failure or failure of schools for disproportionate numbers of children from poor or minority backgrounds are far-ranging. Policy determinations may have far-reaching consequences, considering that school performance and the highest grade level achieved will affect the course of the individual's life. Implied in federal policy is the presumption that we know "why Johnny can't read." Compensatory child-care programs incorporate the premise of environmental pathology both in the home and in the school. Head Start, parent and child centers, developmental child-care centers, and related programs rest on the idea that home environments lack essential ingredients—adequate stimulation, health care and nutrition, or child-rearing technique—causing children to start school with handicaps which are compounded with the passage of time.

Compensatory education for disadvantaged children in public schools has been shaped with deference to state and local control over primary and secondary school policies and decisions. Federal programs exert indirect influence for environmental change by providing additional dollars to be used in educating disadvantaged children. The programs rest on the hypothesis that some measure of school failure is due to inadequate resources and that federal dollars may tilt resources in favor of disadvantaged groups. Within broad federal guidelines, the utilization of the added resources remains in local hands.

Prekindergarten programs have remained largely in the private sector, allowing federal policymakers comparative freedom in designing and implementing programs. However, as preprimary schools gain wider acceptance by public school systems, increasing dependence is being placed on strategies that work through the established school systems.

What it all boils down to is that, presently, the payoffs for early education programs are unknown. Participation in kindergarten has not been found to have a significant impact on later school performance, and payoffs from more structured preschool programs have not been adequately measured. There is no proof that preschool programs work or that most children are either better or worse off outside the home. The theoretical basis for developmental day care centers, nursery schools, and kindergartens is more speculation than hard fact.

However, lack of measurable educational returns should not be equated with lack of attractiveness to parents. Education is generally regarded as a positive social good for all children and accepted as a public responsibility. Parents accept the role of schools in the care, socialization, and education of their children. Other services purchased by affluent parents for their children, such as summer camp or nursery school, have a recognized educational content combined with leisure, entertainment, or babysitting functions and are considered luxuries.

Almost all services for children—nursery school, kindergarten, day care centers, or care for the child at home—include some custodial aspects and some educational inputs. Although there have been some attempts, it is hard to measure how much education each mode includes. Nevertheless, it is far easier to gain public support when the program's primary identification is with education, and the early childhood development debates of the 1960s identified institutional arrangements such as developmental day care centers, nursery schools, and kindergartens with "education," thus increasing their acceptability as public functions.

Public school systems are expanding to reach increasing numbers of three-, four-, and five-year-olds, and this trend is likely to continue as shrinking enrollments at the elementary school level create excess capacity. Universal provision of preschool education has several positive aspects. For one, it is an equalizer. All children attend whether or not their mothers work or have special interest in preschool programs. School systems qualify enrollment by residence and offer more heterogeneity than systems that subsidize attendance of some children but not others. While school systems potentially provide greater integration of peer groups than programs that give preferential access to the poor and disadvantaged, they are far from total solutions. Because of residential patterns, similar racial and income groups tend to be concentrated in single school districts. Poor districts tend to have greater difficulty in raising educational revenues but need costlier remedial services for their children. In addition, the public school system itself has been accused of contributing to learning problems of groups who tend to underachieve. Indeed, some sectors have advocated breaking the monopoly of public schools by offering alternative financing arrangements for education.

Nevertheless, preschool education has been far less controversial than universal child-care programs designed to remove work impediments or subsidize employment of mothers. Such programs are stigmatized because eligibility is presumably a function of economic need or family breakdown, and consequently, they have little appeal to the general public. But the expanded need for child care due to social changes is likely to generate wide consensus justifying government assistance for surrogate care as a "free" social good. Availability of public preprimary schools, which are fast becoming universal, may temper the type of additional programs parents desire. Developmental day care centers may lose appeal when competing with the school system. Also, part-day preschool will saturate the attention span of young children, and parents may desire more informal arrangements for the balance of their child-care needs.

Social trends suggest that increasing populations of three-, four-, and five-year-olds will get more than mere care through public education programs. However, in 1973 close to 2.6 million children under three years old had working mothers, but to date few formal facilities have been provided to care for infants and toddlers. Care of infants and toddlers demands low adult-child ratios and a lot of warm and affectionate attention. The needs of infants and toddlers may be more easily met through home child-care arrangements, and homes are the setting for most care for children of this age. However, in-home arrangements are far more difficult to regulate, and with the exception of care directly paid for by government programs, regulation of care is left to what mothers are willing to accept.

CHAPTER SIX / THE FEDERAL
CHILD-CARE DOLLAR

THE MULTIPLE GOALS

During the decade following the inauguration of the Great Society, federal expenditures for the care and education of preschool-age children have grown from less than $300 million to close to $1.4 billion. The multiple purposes of federal child-care and education programs include both alleviation of poverty and dependency and assistance to working mothers to defray the costs of child care. There are overlaps among categories, but in rough figures about one-fifth of the aid was in the form of tax subsidies for the child-care expenditures of working mothers, and the balance was divided between outlays for compensatory education programs and other services to children of poor working mothers (table 10).

Federal policy relies upon a mixture of direct and indirect approaches to accomplish these goals. In most cases, programs work in partnership with state and local authorities, but there are wide variations in the degree of federal control over program content and thrust. For instance, the Head Start program is a direct federal initiative, and program content, direction, and funding are federal decisions. On the other hand, grants to state and local education agencies under Title I of the Elementary and Secondary School Act leave spending and program decisions to local authorities, within broad general guidelines and regulations controlling expenditures and practices.

TABLE 10. Federal expenditures contributed about $1.4 billion for care and education of preschool children, 1973.

	Expenditures (millions)
TOTAL	$1,392
Education oriented	599
Head Start	402
Elementary and Secondary Education, Title I	97
Other education programs	100
Serving employment of disadvantaged populations	533
Social services	397
WIN	42
Income disregards	80
Model cities	14
Tax subsidies for working mothers	260[1]

[1] Tax exemption not collected by the U.S. Treasury because of deductions.
Sources: U.S. Department of Health, Education, and Welfare; Office of Management and Budget; U.S. Department of Treasury

Several federal efforts focus on removing work impediments for the poor. Social services are provided under the Social Security Act, and every state is required to maintain programs for members of families receiving public assistance. While states have flexibility in determining eligibility for benefits, there are at least some federal checks on the types of services purchased. Institutional child-care services are subject to federal quality guidelines and are supposed to free parents for work or training. State laws regulate whether working welfare mothers who purchase their own unregulated child-care services may include the costs as work-related expenses deductable from income for purposes of calculating welfare payments. The type and quality of care purchased is left solely to the working parent. This practice has been faulted because mothers purchasing services out of a meager AFDC grant are compelled to choose low-cost, low-quality arrangements. The federal role in this type of nonregulated child care is indirect but still significant, since federal outlays cover between 50 and 83 percent of Aid to Families with Dependent Children benefits and the income disregards affect the size of federal welfare expenditures.

TAX CREDITS
The federal government also utilizes tax policy to permit middle-income working mothers to help defray the child-care costs. The government exercises little control over the quality and type of care purchased.

Currently, this assistance for non-poor families represents a relatively small portion of work-related child-care expenditures. Proposals are pending, however, for liberalizing the program to reach an expanded population, meriting examination of the impact of the tax structure on the child-care system, the proposed eligibility criteria, and the level of subsidies.

The purpose and target group for special treatment of child-care expenses under the tax laws has changed substantially since the provision was first instituted in 1954. The original act, which predated most welfare-oriented child-care programs, permitted widows and widowers to deduct up to $600 per year for the care of a dependent child under twelve years old. Working wives were permitted to take the deduction if their family income was less than $4,500. In 1965, the gross income limit was increased to $6,000, the median for family income in that year. The tax deduction remained $600 for one child, but if two or more dependents received care, a total of $900 could be deducted. Relatively few families qualified for or took advantage of this deduction. According to a 1966 study, 245,000 families saved about $26 million in taxes that year.[1]

As the number of working wives and single parents increased, the claims for tax relief to defray the costs of child care mounted. The Revenue Act of 1971 reflected these concerns. The age of qualifying children was raised to fifteen years, and the family income cutoff level was raised from $6,000 to $18,000 a year. In addition, the act allowed taxpayers to cut child-care deductions by fifty cents for each dollar of earnings over $18,000. Thus, child-care deductions were possible for families with incomes up to $27,600, provided the care cost $4,800 or more. Allowable deductions jumped from an annual maximum of $900 to $4,800 for in-home care, even if certain household services were included as part of the child care. Maximum deductions for care rendered outside the household were set at $200 a month for the first child, $300 per month for two children, and $400 a month for three or more dependents.[2]

Provisions in the 1971 tax law precluded payment to other family members and persons residing in the household unless they were specifically hired to provide child care and other services that allow mothers to work. For instance, a taxpayer could deduct the cost of a live-in maid but not payments made to a grandmother providing the same services. The law presumed that services of family members would be available if no payment were made and eliminated the possibility of "paper hires."

The relative merits of in- and out-of-home child care are unclear. Since the care in the child's home tends to be less expensive than educational day care centers, the current provision seems unduly biased, and it may be viewed as a special tax refuge for middle-income families.

If working parents enroll children in preprimary schools, that cost may also be deducted. This may provide a boon to the development of private preprimary education, but public primary schools are universally offered, and after the kindergarten level educational costs may not be deducted.

In 1972, an estimated 1.5 million families deducted $1.0 billion from their taxes for child care and care of incapacitated dependents. This amounted to an actual tax savings of about $224 million, or a rebate of about $147 per family.[3] By 1973, the value of the tax subsidy probably reached $260 million as more families took advantage of the provision.

Tax deductions for child care are utilized primarily by middle-income persons. Lower-income families normally use the minimum standard deduction instead of itemizing allowable deductions. Consequently, a single-parent family with an annual income of $5,000 would probably not realize a tax saving in the purchase of $500 worth of child care for an only child. But a two-parent family with $15,000 earnings might realize a saving of $110 on a $500 expenditure for care of an only child.[4]

The rationale for the child-care deduction policy is that certain costs are involved in generating a second income if young children are part of the family unit. Also, families usually get to keep a smaller portion of second salaries due to progressive income tax policies and payroll taxes. For instance, a man supporting a wife and two children on a $12,500 salary might typically pay a federal income tax of $1,300, or a little more than 11 percent of gross earnings. If his wife earned an additional $5,000, the typical federal tax bite for both of them would rise by $1,076, or about 22 percent of her earnings. Social Security payroll deductions take away another $292. Work costs, plus the costs of the services, including child care, made necessary because the mother was away from home much of the day, would perhaps wipe out total additional earnings. The 1971 Revenue Act provided recognition of work costs of the single parent and working wives by softening the tax burden on these groups.

However, there are rigidities in the deduction allowances, some of which may be construed as inequities. Both parents, or the mother in female-headed households, must work at least three-fourths the full-time equivalent work week in order to qualify. Some mothers may be unable to find full-time work or suitable full-time child care but still have to pay for child care in order to work part time.

A divorced woman whose former husband pays more than 50 percent of the support of their children in her custody cannot claim a tax deduction for child care. Nevertheless, she may be paying for child care in order to work. In this case no one gets the child-care deductions, even though statistics suggest that single mothers suffer great economic hardship.

In 1974, the House Ways and Means Committee proposed a number of changes that would simplify and broaden overall applications of the child-care deductions. These proposals would further liberalize the law to include child-care deductions for parents working part time, full-time students, and working mothers who are separated or divorced but do not claim their children as dependents because the father pays 50 percent or more of the children's support costs. In addition, the law would be changed to remove distinctions between in- and out-of-home care, allowing a maximum annual child-care deduction of $2,400 for the first child and $4,800 for two or more children.[5] These proposed changes recognize special needs and rectify certain inequities in existing laws. About half a million additional families would benefit from tax savings if the above provisions were enacted. It is estimated that about four of every five families would be in the $7,000 to $20,000 annual income bracket.

A measure liberalizing the child-care deduction was tacked onto the 1975 tax cut bill, but reforms suggested by the House Ways and Means proposal were omitted. Starting in 1976, the $4,800 maximum child care deduction becomes applicable to families whose annual income did not exceed $35,000, with partial deductions phasing out when annual family income reached $44,600.

As indirect financial and social service policies have provided child care for the working poor, tax provisions have moved in the direction of aiding those with less pressing financial needs. The trend over the past two decades toward broadening eligibility suggests that univeral tax deductions for working mothers may soon be adopted. Such a provision would essentially benefit upper-income families. Low-income families can ill afford large outlays, even if income tax benefits offset about one-fifth the total cost. Whether equity would be served by offering universal tax deductions for child care remains questionable.

The effects of tax policies, in addition to the obvious loss of tax dollars, are elusive. The provision benefits mothers who already work. There is no evidence that women have flocked into the labor force to take advantage of past changes in tax consideration of child-care costs. But tax policies that favor purchased services may influence mothers' choice to work, tipping the scales in favor of outside employment.

REMOVING OBSTACLES TO EMPLOYMENT

One of the aims of federal child-care policy is to defray part of work connected expenses. As noted, these programs are of little value to low earners. But the child-care needs of mothers on welfare are of special concern. Limited earning potential makes the decision about whether or not to work more difficult, especially when child-care costs are high.

In 1973, there were 3.2 million preschool-age children living in families with an annual income of less than $4,000 and an additional 2.2 million children less than six years old living in families with an annual income between $4,000 and $7,000. Welfare supported 2.6 million of these preschoolers, and 3.1 million were counted among the poor in 1973. Federal child-care programs are centered around these children. Only three in ten have working mothers, and broadening child-care services may free more mothers to increase family income and reduce dependency.

SOCIAL SERVICES AND
DAY CARE

A number of programs have been undertaken in the last decade to induce poor parents to work by providing safe custody and other social services for their children. The federal government first got into the business of financing social services following the adoption of the 1956 amendments to the Social Security Act. The law made provision of social services an integral part of public assistance and authorized a 50 percent sharing of social service costs. The federal share was boosted to 75 percent by 1962 amendments and the Secretary of HEW was given the responsibilty of prescribing mandatory social services.

Starting as a modest effort, federal contribution to social services became a mutibillion dollar undertaking following the 1967 Social Security amendments, which directed states to provide child care, foster parent care, family planning, legal services, and health-related services to meet the needs of families and children. States could provide services purchased from public and private agencies to current, as well as former or potential, AFDC recipients and to a broad spectrum of other poor or near-poor persons. This broad eligibility greatly expanded the clientele for the services. It also made federal funds available to states for programs that had formerly depended almost exclusively on state and local resources and provided opportunities to charge other outlays to "social services." The rapid expansion of federal social service costs represented in large part federal refinancing of existing services formerly paid for by states, rather than an increase of this aid. The 1967 amendments authorizing open-ended expenditures were regarded as manna for the states. Federal outlays rose from $230 million in 1968 to $1.9 billion in 1972.[6] Congress viewed the funds as relief for hard-pressed states, but balked at the prospect of annual trebling of costs. With administration prompting, in October 1972 Congress limited annual social services expenditures to $2.5 billion.[7]

Having shut off the money spigot, the HEW administrators tried to issue appropriate regulations in line with the funding constraints. They attempted to limit mandatory services to family planning, foster care, and child protection. Placed on the optional list were employment-related child care and day care for the mentally retarded. Apparently, the promulgators of the proposed regulations despaired of providing "free" day care as a means to reduce welfare rolls, the prevailing rhetoric notwithstanding. Though Congress tightened the purse, it refused to sanction the new regulations consistent with the fund limitations.

Provision of day care was a focal point in the fight to keep availability of social services loosely regulated. The open-ended authorization, plus the lack of specificity of state plans requesting federal grants, obscured the details of what these dollars actually purchased. Unlike other social services, the bulk of day care was purchased from the private vendors instead of public agencies. However, not all the apparent expansion of child-care expenditures was real. In fiscal year 1972, several states that had subsidized child care through income disregards or other programs switched in order to take advantage of higher federal matching provided under the federal social services funding.[8] While the total social service expenditures rose nearly fivefold between 1969 and 1973, outlays for day care grew twice as rapidly (chart 9). The numbers of child-care years charged to social service accounts increased from an estimated 43,000 in 1969 to 410,000 in 1973, as the average federal cost per child-care year rose from about $800 in 1969 to $968 in 1973.

Outlays for day care were not necessarily commensurate with services provided, as many slots which were paid for by welfare agencies went unfilled. On-site reviews in Washington indicated that the slots paid for exceeded the actual average daily attendance at day care sites by one-third.[9] In Dallas, Texas, it was found that over a five-month period, average daily attendance was 26 percent below the number of day care center slots contracted. About 11 percent of contracted day care home slots remained unfilled in Dallas and Houston.[10] A General Accounting Office report indicated the average attendance in six California child-care centers was 68 percent. Average attendance in 26 Pennsylvania centers was 72 percent.[11]

Social service funds purchase child care in the child's home, in family day care homes, or in day care centers. However, few supposedly state-approved child-care arrangements could meet federal standards. Even states with long traditions of child-care services fall short of meeting licensing, staffing, fire, health, safety, and other federal standards for day care centers. For instance, California has run day care centers as a part of the educational system since they were established under the 1942 Lanham Act. Between 1946 and 1968, these facilities were financed totally with state funds. The 1967 amendments to the Social Security Act allowed purchase of services by the state welfare agency from the state department of education. Financ-

CHART 9. Outlays for child care and other social services, 1969–1973.

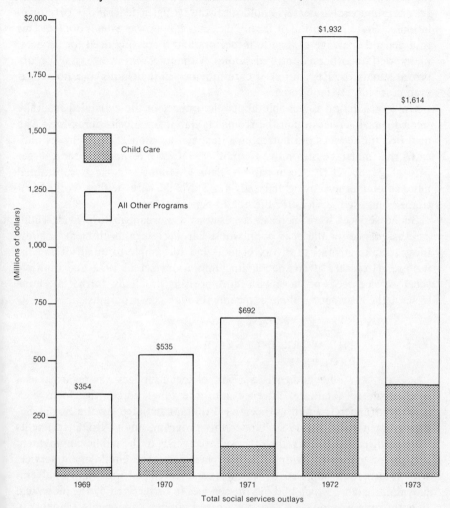

Source: U.S. Congress, Joint Economic Committee, *Open-Ended Federal Matching of State Social Service Expenditure Authorized Under the Public Assistance Titles of the Social Security Act* (Washington: Government Printing Office, 1972), p. 6; and U.S. Department of Health, Education, and Welfare, "Social Services Under Title IV, Part A of the Social Security Act: Child Care—Federal Share of Costs, Average Number of Children, and Average Cost per Child—Fiscal Year 1972 and 1973," February 6, 1973 (unpublished table).

75

ing of centers was taken over by the federal funds, but only a relative handful of state-operated centers could meet the stringent federal day care regulations.[12] State regulation of family day care homes was even more lax. Due to a general shortage of license inspectors and a pressing need for services, many welfare offices approved homes without checking licensing or approval standards. Regulation of care provided in the child's own home was even more loosely monitored.

Only speculation is possible about the impact of the expanded federally funded social services upon the recipients' labor force behavior. Many who qualified for services did not receive financial assistance. Spot checks indicated that marriage or a move to another state was responsible for a larger percentage of AFDC terminations than obtaining a job. A substantial number of mothers using federally funded child care neither worked nor trained, but used services for their child-benefit value.[13]

Social services were increasingly used as a mechanism to provide child-care assistance for the near poor, whose earnings were insufficient to allow them to take advantage of tax benefits but too ample to qualify them for welfare. However, given the funding limitations set in 1972 and multiple social service needs of those with more pressing problems, further attempts to serve the near poor will have to come through new programs.

THE WORK INCENTIVE PROGRAM

While child care as a part of social services was regarded as a mechanism to facilitate entrance into the labor force, the focus was sharpened under the Work Incentive Program initiated by the Social Security amendments of 1967. Under this program, adult AFDC recipients were required to be referred by the welfare agency to the public employment service for manpower training or job placement. The employment service, with information supplied by caseworkers, developed an "individual employability plan," which laid out the services to be received by the individual in both training and social services areas. Training components available to those not directly placed in a job included on-the-job training (OJT), public service employment, and institutional training.

While in training, the participants received a $30 a month incentive payment in addition to the AFDC grant. Subsequently, participants could keep $30 a month, plus a third of additional earnings, with offsets for child care if not provided by WIN. The program was financed by a federal-state shared costs plan under which federal sources paid 80 percent of manpower and training costs (administered through the employment services), and 75 percent of social services costs (delivered through welfare agencies). The 1971 Talmadge amendments raised the federal funding share to 90 percent for both manpower and supportive social services.

By 1974, several major policy changes were proposed for the WIN program. Reliance upon training to enhance employability dwindled, and emphasis was placed upon immediate employment. The new WIN would require persons to register with manpower agencies for job placement services concurrently with their application for welfare benefits.[14]

Although most AFDC families are headed by single females, priorities for WIN services reflect other considerations. Mothers of children under six years old are not required to participate in the program. Women with preschool-age children can and often do volunteer for job placement services, but they are free to drop out of the program without fear of sanctions. The order in which registrants are referred places unemployed fathers first, followed by mothers who volunteer, other mothers and pregnant women under nineteen years old who are required to register, and dependent children over sixteen years old who are not in school or training.

In fiscal year 1973, four out of ten male WIN participants were placed in jobs, compared with only one in ten women. For multiple reasons, including service needs, inadequate job skills and work experience, job discrimination, competition for available jobs, and a generally soft labor market for women workers, welfare mothers were unable to land jobs with adequate wages to support them and their children. In addition, the public employment service itself may contribute to the poor results: women have sometimes not been told of employment opportunities for upwardly mobile apprenticeship jobs because those are customarily considered male jobs.[15]

Other factors also contributed to job placement problems. About one-third of total women registrants volunteered to participate, and these volunteers could leave the program and return to welfare at any time without sanctions. Also, a woman's mandatory registration status was more apt to change due to pregnancy or collapse of a child-care arrangement. Almost half of the women accepted into the WIN program were in orientation, training, or just plain waiting, compared to only 7 percent of men. Suitable job placements and combinations of services are apparently more difficult to arrange for women. Additionally, WIN administrators who experienced high drop-out rates among women volunteers tended to downgrade volunteers' chances for placement and concentrated their efforts on more likely candidates.[16]

Even when WIN did place its women enrollees, the results were discouraging. Their average hourly wage rate in 1973 was $1.87, compared with $2.58 for men, and one out of eleven women entered jobs at less than the federal minimum wage rate of $1.60 per hour. The average hourly wage rate of $1.87 yielded about $320 in monthly earnings, assuming full time work of forty hours a week. The first thirty dollars, and one-third of additional earnings, could be deducted before any welfare benefit was reduced. Work-connected expenses, plus payroll and income taxes, further reduced the amount that could be subtracted from welfare payments to about $140 a month. This amount was barely sufficient to cover the cost of day care for one child in a federally approved facility. If two or more children were involved, day care costs alone would have exceeded the total welfare "savings" to the government; these calculations did not include outlays for other social services that averaged nearly $300 per family in fiscal 1973.

Child Care Delivered under WIN. To maintain welfare eligibility, mothers with children of school age must have registered for WIN and accepted child care that met federal regulations. If alternative kinds of child care were available, the participant could choose the type she preferred. The mother could not refuse child-care services and stay home if suitable child care were available. Mothers of younger children could volunteer for the program and be provided with services, but they had the option of leaving WIN at any time.

In fiscal 1973, a monthly average of 58,000 women were provided subsidized day care for 126,000 children; nearly half of these children were younger than age six. The types of care provided varied by age of children. One of every three children under six years was placed in day care facilities. While there was no record that children under six years old were left unattended, nearly one of every nine older children was left without care while the mother was training or working (table 11).

According to a 1972 study, three-fourths of WIN participants with dependent children required child-care services. The program financed all costs for more than four-fifths of participants requiring child care. Cost of in-home babysitting arrangements averaged $11 per week, while center care averaged close to $14 per week.[17] Mothers participating in WIN child care-arrangements averaged 2.3 children, and the costs per family therefore exceeded average outlays per child.

A 1972 study conducted in six cities compared child-care needs and delivery for WIN participants and non-WIN AFDC recipients. It found that WIN participants were far less likely to need child care services, "need" being defined as the presence of a child under fifteen years old with no other adult available to provide supervision. In WIN families, almost three of every five children were between six and fifteen years old, and less than one-fifth of the children were under three years old. Forty-eight percent of non-

TABLE 11. Child-care arrangements of WIN participants, fiscal 1973.

Arrangements	Total	Children under 6	Children 6–14
TOTAL (monthly average)	126,259	57,447	68,582
Percent	100.0	100.0	100.0
Own Home	43.1	43.4	42.6
Father	2.1	1.4	2.5
Other relative	20.0	21.1	18.9
Nonrelative	15.4	14.8	15.9
Homemaker	.6	.5	.6
Relatives' homes	11.0	12.3	9.7
Day care facility	25.0	34.6	16.7
Family day care home	13.5	16.9	10.5
Group day care home	1.1	1.4	.9
Day care center	9.3	15.5	5.0
Other	20.9	8.6	31.1
Training only while children in school	7.2	1.0	12.5
Self	4.8	—	8.8
Other	7.4	5.8	7.7

Source: Derived from U.S. Department of Health, Education and Welfare, Social and Rehabilitation Service, NCSS Report E-4, 1972 and 1973.
Note: Details may not add to total because of incomplete reporting.

WIN AFDC recipients had dependents between six and fifteen years of age and 28 percent cared for children less than three years old. WIN participants made fewer arrangements in formal facilities compared to non-WIN participants receiving social services. Considering that the government was footing the bill, it is not surprising that WIN child-care arrangements were more costly on the average than those that were paid for by non-WIN mothers, despite the higher age of children and the mode of care selected.[18]

The child-care arrangement reflected a number of conditions. In many areas, formal child-care facilities were nonexistent or failed to meet federal requirements. Also, WIN staff practices affected the choice of care. In some communities, the WIN staff regarded the mother's selection as the best method for insuring a satisfactory child-care arrangement. Other staffs believed that they knew best and tried to impose their preferences on participants. Some projects were filled by unemployed men and women with no children under six years old, and thus had few participants who needed costly child-care arrangements. Some WIN programs placed limits on the amount paid for child care. Still others relied on child-care arrangements not from the WIN budget but from other federally funded programs.

Altogether, an estimated 22 percent of the child-care services used in fiscal 1973 by WIN mothers was charged to Head Start, Model Cities, and other programs.[19] The incidence of child-care cost paid by other programs will undoubtedly decline. The 1971 amendments increased the federal share of WIN child-care costs from 75 to 90 percent of the total. This reduced the comparative advantage to states of financing WIN-related child care out of other budgets.

Child-care services under WIN were also purchased under the "income disregard" in thirty-one states. This system allowed mothers to make their own arrangements and deduct the costs from their earnings without affecting the AFDC payment. It was charged that such arrangements were usually "low quality" and promoted payment for services provided free of cost by relatives. On the other hand, the method has been commended because mothers chose the most convenient setting to meet their work and training demands free of institutional interference.

Some states used a voucher system allowing mothers to contract with a caregiver, and the welfare agency reimbursed the provider for services rendered. A study of the day care voucher used by WIN indicated that the required paperwork created problems for the client, caregiver, and welfare agency. There were frequent delays in payment. As a result, the supply of available child-care facilities was reduced because some providers of day care were discouraged by complicated paperwork and could not afford to wait for delayed reimbursement.[20]

Uncertain Outlook for WIN. Congress's declining confidence in WIN's potential was probably reflected in its trimming of the WIN budget for fiscal 1974 to $340 million, $194 million less than the amount requested by the administration. The 1975 budget request did not anticipate further expansion of the program, and the emphasis remained on job placement rather than training.

The future of WIN depends largely upon societal views on whether women without adequate means of support should be compelled to work in menial low-paying occupations as a condition for income support and whether this helps reduce welfare rolls. The traditional practice of grudging support for welfare families and of making dependency at least uncomfortable is being challenged. Forcing AFDC mothers to work elicits emotional responses. Proponents argue that the majority of non-AFDC mothers with school-age children work and over a third work full time. To expect the same from AFDC mothers should not be considered "punishment." The argument fails to consider the fact that other women seek work voluntarily, while welfare mothers would be coerced into taking jobs.

FOR WHOM SHOULD UNCLE
SAM BABYSIT?

Programs to increase the labor force participation of disadvantaged and welfare populations raise a number of policy questions. Should programs be designed to help those with the greatest needs, or should they be directed to families who are capable of self-sufficiency with only a marginal amount of outside assistance? Given an unfavorable prognosis for achieving self-sufficiency, how much pressure should be put on dependent mothers of preschool-age children to place their child in another's care and to accept employment? Should everyone be offered the same types of care? Should mothers have options of picking child development programs over care by a grandmother or other low-cost option?

Even though many in the disadvantaged and welfare populations have child-care problems, there is great variation in the ease with which these problems can be solved. It is easier to provide care to school-age children than preschool-age children, and more can be served with limited resources. Federal policymakers have been reluctant to pressure mothers of preschool-age children to accept employment, partly because of social values which favor care of young children by mothers and partly because the prognosis for self-sufficiency is not promising.

Many poor families are headed by women who have low earning potential even when child-care problems are alleviated or removed. It is doubtful whether it is cost effective to provide these women with child care and all the other services needed in order to maintain employment, especially if more than one preschool-age child is involved. For these families, the promise of reduced welfare expenditures will not be realized, considering the increased costs of social services needed to maintain employment. However, combinations of earnings, welfare supplements, and social services may raise the overall standard of living, and perhaps this goal should be substituted for cost effectiveness criteria.

It is unclear whether current methods for dispensing child care, especially under social services, actually encourage labor force participation. State welfare agencies do not maintain information showing how many mothers go to work as the result of child care or how many worked before services were available using other child-care arrangements. There is also little hard data to show any correlation between the cost of child care and benefits to the child, thus weakening the case for choosing the most expensive child-care option because it is best for the child. An alternative strategy would be to spread limited resources to help as many families as possible. There is a need for better techniques and standards of assessment in this regard if the impact of child care on the self-sufficiency of welfare and disadvantaged populations is to be known.

Finally, although some welfare-related child care reaches the near poor, many marginally self-sufficient families fall into a "no man's land," with incomes too high to qualify for welfare-related programs but too low to benefit from tax credits. A variety of bills have been introduced to make welfare-type child care available to the near poor but have ultimately failed because of the presumed high price tag. The potential costs of aiding the near poor have been inflated by the emphasis on developmental-center-based programs. Perhaps policymakers should examine alternate strategies that would assist working mothers and raise family income but would do so at a cost that is more politically acceptable.

CHAPTER SEVEN / HEAD START—
FIGHTING POVERTY WITH EARLY
EDUCATION

CREATION AND
TRANSITION

A concerted attack on poverty was a major hallmark of the Great Society. The Office of Economic Opportunity was created to represent the interests of the poor and to fund antipoverty programs as part of the "War on Poverty." Early remedial intervention was advocated by numerous educators, and Head Start, a preschool program designed to break the "cycle of poverty" by augmenting deficient environments with enrichment programs, became a cornerstone of the antipoverty effort and the most popular antipoverty program.[1]

Head Start grants were disbursed through community action agencies (CAAs) for program operation by schools, churches, nonprofit agencies, and by the CAAs themselves. Parents were to influence Head Start policies and operations via parent advisory boards. Confrontation between school superintendents and advisory boards resulted in OEO's downgrading the advisory board's role to a consultative one in 1966, and a year later Congress placed community action agencies under the control of elected officials. The same law also exhibited confidence in the Head Start concept by creating

83

Follow Through, in order to test methods for extending Head Start gains to the early primary grades.

With the election of a Republican administration, official enthusiasm for the Office of Economic Opportunity dimmed. President Richard Nixon favored initially confining OEO to the role of initiator and "incubator" of experimental programs and, before his forced resignation, attempted to terminate the antipoverty agency. Since Head Start had already proven its popularity, President Nixon recommended the transfer of Head Start to HEW in order to "strengthen it by association with a wide range of other early development programs within the Department."[2] On July 1, 1969, the Office of Child Development was created in the Office of the Secretary and assigned operation of Head Start. Four years later, the Office of Child Development became part of the newly formed Office of Human Development.

Despite the administrative changes at the top, Head Start maintained essentially the same program delivery apparatus through community action agencies.[3] As of 1973, regional child development offices made grants to CAAs which ran the program or selected delegate grantees to operate projects. Sponsors of the projects were distributed in 1969 and 1970 as follows:

Program operator	Summer 1969	Full-year 1970
Total	100%	100%
Local CAA	36	48.5
Public school	51	22.5
Private nonprofit group	2	9
Church	2	4
Other	7	9
Nonreported	2	7

The dismantling of OEO during the 1970s brought the demise of a number of CAAs. As the result, the number of agencies whose sole function was to operate Head Start projects increased, but the exact number is not recorded.

ADMINISTRATIVE
STRUCTURE

Head Start operated summer programs; full-year, full-day programs; and full-year, part-day programs. The part-day program averaged four hours a day for nine months a year. Full-year, full-day programs operated an average of eight hours a day, eleven months per year.

Initial enthusiasm for Head Start ran high, but in light of later, more calm appraisal, it appears naive. Vacant classrooms and vacationing teachers were mobilized in the summer of 1965 to serve 561,000 children, and they handled 573,000 children in the following summer. A 1966 study found that benefits gained from summer programs faded quickly and that "quick one-stop opportunity simply is not enough."[4] The realization that children could not make dramatic gains in eight weeks was instrumental in deemphasizing the summer program in favor of a full-year program. Due to budgetary constraints, however, total enrollment dropped because of the higher costs encountered in running full-year projects (chart 10).

CHART 10. Head Start enrollments shifted from summer to full-year programs.

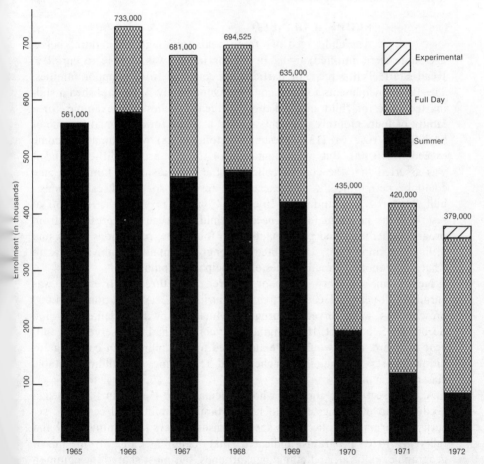

Source: U.S. Department of Health, Education and Welfare, Office of Child Development, "Head Start Statistics—Fiscal Years 1968-1974" (unpublished tables), and Sar A. Levitan, The Great Society's Poor Law (Baltimore: The Johns Hopkins Press, 1969), p. 139.

Although policymakers repeatedly emphasized Head Start's role as an enrichment program and urged grantees to tap non-Head Start resources to provide day care services, Head Start projects doubled as day care centers providing full-day services for between a third and a fourth of enrolled children.[5] Some projects only accepted children of working mothers. In neighborhoods where centers provided full-day care, they were likely to serve children of nonworking mothers. Also, because close to two-thirds of Head Start children had at least one brother or sister under six years old, working mothers with children in full-day, full-year programs had to make other day care arrangements for siblings too young or too old to participate.

SCOPE AND NEED

Any child aged two to six years (although few children below age three were enrolled) living in a poor family was eligible to enroll in Head Start. Ten percent of participants could be from nonpoor families. The 1972 amendments to the Economic Opportunity Act established a sliding fee scale for children from more affluent families. For example: for a family of four, monthly payments started at $2.50 for an annual income of $4,700 and rose to $135 (presumably total costs) when annual income exceeded $10,100. But implementation of the law proved difficult, and it was asserted that the cost of collecting the fees, assuming family income could be determined, would exceed the revenue, so the "fiscal responsibility" effort was abandoned.[6] In effect, Congress reversed the trade-off of reserving the program for the neediest children because of pressures from program operators and participants, who found new regulations costly and difficult to implement. Undoubtedly, Congress remained ambivalent as to what the economic circumstances of participants should be.

Nearly one of every five poor children aged three to five years was enrolled full-year in Head Start centers during 1972. An additional 174,000 preschoolers were served in programs financed by the Elementary and Secondary School Act. If all eligible poor children had been served in a full-year program, costs would have amounted to $2.8 billion, not counting additional costs for training teachers and renovating or building suitable classroom facilities.

A cross-section of children who participated in Head Start revealed a needy group of youngsters who lacked family stability and economic security. Information collected in special census surveys for summer 1969 and full-year 1970 programs indicated that children came from mixed geographic, cultural, and ethnic backgrounds, but most shared the common background of poverty and they tended to come from large families (table 12).

TABLE 12. Characteristics of Head Start children and families, 1969–1970.

Characteristics	Summer 1969	Full-year 1970
Ethnic/cultural group		
Total	100%	100%
White	43	26
Black	37	51
Spanish surnamed	13	15
American Indian and Eskimo	1	4
Oriental and other	2	1
Not reported	4	3
Age of children		
Total	100	100
3 years or less	6	19
4 years old	20	44
5 years old	41	31
6 years old and older	32	3
Not reported	1	2
Father living with child	75	62
Employment of parents		
Father employed	86	80
Mother employed	25	38
Family received public welfare	25	39
Median family size, persons	6.4	6.6
Median family income	$3,770	$3,350

Source: U.S. Department of Health, Education, and Welfare, Office of Child Development, *Project Head Start 1969–1970: A Descriptive Report of Programs and Participants* (Washington: Office of Child Development, 1972), pp. 59–66.

Home settings varied, with 40 percent of children living in rural areas and 60 percent in urban areas. Some rural children were located in town centers, some used the transportation provided for public schools, and some rode special mini buses to get to Head Start centers. But transportation remained a problem in rural areas, and many children were denied access to Head Start because they were too distantly located.

Head Start children clearly constituted a disadvantaged segment of the population, but they were not necessarily the poorest children. Community social service agency referrals were frequently a source of recruitment, which did not assure that the neediest children were reached, and income criteria were not always verified. Some projects did not have systematic checks on income eligibility and took the parents' word that children were eligible. Parental involvement in recruiting and screening was found generally lacking.

Guidelines proscribed segregation by race, directing that enrollment reflect the racial and ethnic distribution in the geographic area served.

Nonetheless, centers tended to serve homogeneous groups, reflecting segregated housing patterns, geographic isolation (Indians on reservations), and parental biases, which prevented children's participation in integrated facilities. Allocation of resources to the neediest also tended to reinforce racial segregation. A bill to expand Head Start services and provide subsidized day care to a broader economic range passed Congress in 1971, but it was vetoed by President Nixon on the grounds that the proposed annual $2.1 billion outlay for child care was fiscally irresponsible, administratively unworkable, and had family-weakening implications.[7]

The economic and racial homogeneity of Head Start clientele continued to plague the program. But in light of past difficulties in recruiting children from racially heterogeneous areas and the persisting racial segregation in housing patterns, it can be surmised that expanded eligibility might have achieved broader economic enrollment in Head Start, but not racial integration.

PROGRAM COMPONENTS

Early childhood education, health and psychological services, nutrition, and social services constituted the core of Head Start operations. The program attempted to strengthen its effectiveness through career development of staff, volunteer services, and parent involvement in all components.

Education. Education is the central focus of Head Start. Performance standards called for a ratio of one teacher and two teacher aides to serve approximately fifteen children. In 1972, the professional staff to child ratio was one to twelve, and the adult to child ratio was one to two (counting volunteers)—half a lap to sit on per child.

Four of every five Head Start staff members were assigned to teaching and the related functions of program administration, social services, and special services such as speech therapy. The remaining fifth were engaged in delivering medical and dental services, preparing meals, maintaining the premises, and transporting children.

Classroom activities were the central focus of the program. However, the initial goal of enabling poor children to catch up with middle-class peers was modified to that of providing children with a learning environment and varied experiences to help them develop a degree of social competence appropriate for their ages and stages of development. Head Start emphasis on child development, including self-esteem and social skills, followed traditional nursery school practices, but with perhaps bigger and better-educated staffs and certainly with greater concentrations of disadvantaged children.

Language development received some attention. Physical examinations identified health defects, including hearing difficulties, brain dysfunction, or other impediments to normal speech development. The program was sensitive to the fact that about one-fourth of the children were either bilingual or spoke a language other than English. Head Start was also sensitive to the controversy over "correct" English and black dialect. Head Start's official stance was to reject the prevailing school practice of attempting to correct dialects and was, instead, to urge staff to teach proficiency in both dialects.[8] Whether this permissive approach best served the interests of the children is questionable. It may have ill prepared them for primary schools which lack linguistic broad mindedness and future employers who may discriminate against persons whose "dialect" departs from the norm.

Aside from raising controversy about the "correct" pedagogical approaches to the learning problems of Head Start children, some studies cast doubt on the attainment of program goals. The definitive evaluation of Head Start is still lacking, although several attempts have been made to appraise the impact of the program. Possibly the most ambitious study was conducted in 1969 by Westinghouse Learning Corporation on former Head Start participants who had advanced to the first three grades. The study concluded that long-term impacts of the summer program were negligible and that even children who attended full-year projects in the deep South or core cities performed only slightly better than their peers.[9]

The study has been criticized on the grounds that it was narrowly focused, that it did not distinguish effective from ineffective programs, that the sample was not representative, and that the measurement instruments were culturally biased and poorly designed. Critics also pointed out that possible spillover effects in the community or the impacts of returning to poverty environments after leaving Head Start were not assessed.[10] Other interpretations concluded that peer groups tended to catch up because kindergarten or the first grade produced equalizing intellectual spurts in children who could not attend Head Start. Also, the potential impact of Head Start may not have been realized because of poor implementation.[11]

Later monitoring assessments indicated that the educational component of Head Start was more successfully implemented than most other aspects of the program. Program quality varied considerably, however, with some program grantees—in Chicago, for instance—exceeding program performance standards in every aspect and others failing in all aspects of performance.[12] There was no evidence that this identification of superior programs measured by performance standards was utilized to implement programs elsewhere or that differences in program implementation did, in fact, affect children's development in some measurable way.

Planned variation in Head Start was limited to a three-year program funded for fiscal years 1969 through 1972 to test the effect of varying educational techniques. From April 1973 on, local Head Start project operators were authorized to implement variations in standard program format, including incorporating specially structured educational models. While reliance on local decisionmaking may be desirable, the wisdom of overlaying ongoing programs with educational "models" may be questioned. Do children learn more in some situations because of differences in teacher performance and the mix of peers, because of *esprit de corps,* or because of other nonquantifiable, nonpackageable factors? A successful teaching "model" may fall flat when used in other situations in which nonquantifiable ingredients are missing. What works in some situations may fail in others. Teaching models may provide helpful tools, but they do not erect the building by themselves and they are not appropriate in all situations. Accordingly, the stress on "models" may have represented a "cop out" on the part of the feds, i.e., a lack of determination to agree on program goals rather than an attempt to encourage diversity and local choice. If a traveler does not know where he is going, any road will do.

Nutrition. Inattentive or listless children may be hungry or poorly nourished. Working on the premise that "the child is what he eats," Head Start has attempted to improve the nutrition of children and their families through a variety of methods. In 1970, about 98 percent of full-year centers served lunch and at least one other meal; three meals were served at the majority of centers, with the mothers occasionally or frequently joining their children at meals. As a rule, due deference was paid to the social and cultural dietary customs of the children.[13]

Head Start provided the major source of nutrition to a substantial proportion of participants, which had the beneficial effect of reducing the demands on the family food budget.[14] For the most part, meals were well-planned, and they met performance benchmarks of providing from one-half to one-third of the children's daily food intake.

Beneficial as they may have been, the nutrition efforts were not without problems. In 1972, program monitors found that some centers relied too heavily on starches, and some wasted food because they did not adjust purchases to account for absenteeism or for the children who were being fed at home. Some Head Start centers were not successful in introducing sound dietary patterns, and many centers placed low priority on parent and child nutritional education.[15] However, primary nutritional problems of Head Start families stem from insufficient funds to purchase higher priced proteins, fresh fruits, and vegetables. Considerable economic and social changes beyond the scope of Head Start capabilities may be necessary to substantially change eating patterns.

Medical and Dental Care. The aspect which most differentiates Head Start from conventional nursery schools is its comprehensive effort to screen children for medical and dental deficiencies and to provide necessary remedial care. In addition to diagnosing and remedying current health defects, the program attempts to improve future health through preventive immunizations and flouride treatments, health education of child and parent, and the introduction of Head Start families to health care delivery systems available on a continuing basis.[16]

In addition to direct hiring of health care personnel and purchasing of care, Head Start tapped other available funding and delivery resources, including Medicaid, neighborhood health centers, maternal and child health grant projects, and other local government or private health care programs.[17] Medicaid guidelines permit early and periodic screening, diagnosis, and treatment of eligible children, including medical and dental treatment and preventive measures available through Head Start. To take advantage of this provision, Head Start has directed maximum utilization of Medicaid resources. The Office of Child Development, together with HEW's Medical Services Administration, launched a pilot program in approximately 200 Head Start projects to provide Medicaid-financed services to eligible children under six years old, including siblings of Head Start enrollees and other non-Head Start participants eligible for Medicaid services.[18] Accordingly, modification of health services and practices to better serve the poor constituted one significant impact of the program.[19]

Almost all children received physical and/or dental examinations. About two-fifths of the children examined had medical or dental problems, and most of these received treatment. Dental cavities, found in half the children, were the most common problem, but about one in ten examined children suffered from anemia, one in twenty had hearing and vision deficiencies, and about 1 percent tested positively for tuberculosis.[20]

Preventive medicine delivered through Head Start channeled children to public health clinics for immunizations which met school system requirements and may have prevented crippling and contagious disease. Most children who entered the full-year program were immunized by the end of the school year.[21] Some of these health services were, of course, available from other federal-state programs, and many Head Start children might have been served even without the program. Without Head Start, however, care might have been provided in a less timely fashion, and some children might not have been reached at all.

Evaluation of the Head Start demonstration project, which delivered the health care component of Head Start on a limited national basis in 1971 and 1972, illustrated some problems experienced by Head Start programs generally. Federal health care programs are fragmented, and program administrators lack incentives to coordinate private as well as public services, stymieing delivery of comprehensive services. Availability of resources in a community is no guarantee that Head Start clientele would participate.[22]

A small proportion of Head Start projects offered psychological services, but these services invariably received low priority because of either budgetary constraints or lack of access to trained personnel.[23] The service was, however, necessary, since one in twenty-five Head Start children was afflicted with behavior or learning problems, mental retardation, or psychiatric disorders.[24] The 1974 requirements that handicapped children constitute 10 percent of Head Start enrollment are likely to change program needs and perhaps upgrade psychological services, if funds are allocated for the added needs.

Parent Participation. Head Start guidelines require parent participation in several program aspects, including (1) planning and operation; (2) designing supportive parent activities; and (3) participating as paid and volunteer program employees.

Policy advisory committees were the primary vehicle for obtaining parent contributions to program planning.[25] Early in the history of Head Start, conflicts diluted the advisory committees' powers, leaving them only consultative roles in planning and approving program proposals and budgets, selection of staff, fund raising, and designing parent programs. The existence of parent policy advisory committee groups does not indicate whether these are informed bodies or "rubber stamp" committees and whether their recommendations are followed or ignored.

In 1970, four of every five centers employed parents, mostly on a volunteer basis. Less than 1 percent of Head Start parents were on project payrolls in 1970, although about one-sixth of paid staff members had children in the program and the children of an additional 15 percent had participated previously. Although almost all parent employment was in low-paying aide roles, an increasing percentage had gained professional positions, indicating some upgrading of staff. An increasing percentage of parents retained their jobs in Head Start projects long after their children had "graduated," limiting opportunities for parents of more recent program enrollees.

The extent to which parent involvement influenced project policy or enhanced other program components has been disputed. Involved parents were found to have children with higher IQ and achievement scores; but these results probably reflected a combination of parent interest and interaction and freedom from health, transportation, and family impediments, rather than benefits which accrued from participation.[26] Employment in Head Start may have supplemented family income, but annual salary levels have been low due to budget limitations, concentration in non-professional positions, and the fact that most projects operate about nine months out of the year.

Evaluation of parent involvement in parent committees, parent councils, and parent-teacher interaction suggests that there is considerable room for improvement. Parent education relating to health and nutrition components has also been weak. However, parent involvement has had little relationship to successful implementation of other program components. Instead, analysis points to leadership and professionalism in the administrative component as the keystone of program success.[27]

A great deal of the parent participation in Head Start projects involved volunteers who performed a multitude of essential Head Start tasks. Ideally, volunteers were recruited from a broad range of backgrounds to deliver services on a communitywide basis under the coordination of a Head Start staff member. However, monitoring reports indicated overall weakness in recruitment efforts, training, staff supervision, and internal evaluation of volunteer efforts.

Training and Career Development. Caring for other people's children has traditionally been a low-paying, low-status job. Given the widely held view that "anyone can take care of kids," early childhood development practitioners are still struggling to gain public recognition of their professional status similar to that accorded to teachers. Head Start aides, mostly recruited from poverty homes, faced much more severe problems of occupational status and pay. Placed in teacher's aide and other non-professional positions, without further training, many aides were left in dead-end jobs.

In order to professionalize employment in Head Start, Congress earmarked $19.1 million for training and technical assistance in 1973. Colleges and universities were contracted to examine Head Start projects and to set up training schedules. In addition to lectures and workshops, the Head Start program subsidized college and university training for Head Start employees. This training occasionally led to credentials such as an Associate of Arts degree. Between 1967 and 1973, 25,000 Head Start employees received some college training, 12,000 for credit; and about 1,000 earned degrees.[28]

Starting in 1974, training focused on a new diploma: the Child Development Associate (CDA). Designed by the Office of Child Development, it is awarded on the basis of demonstrated competencies. A private nonprofit CDA consortium composed of child education and development specialists provided assessment and credentialing criteria. Half the training was supervised field work; academic work was integrated with in-service experience, and associated colleges and training institutions offered credit for CDA training. If the new associate degree wins acceptance, it might reinforce the professional self-image of Head Start employees and provide trained manpower for other preprimary programs. However, with the ever-tightening job market among college-trained teachers, competition for preprimary education positions will be sharp, and credentials battles will likely ensue.

PROGRAM COSTS

The federal government contributed four-fifths of program costs, and local sources provided 20 percent, usually in kind rather than in cash. Between 1965 and 1973, the federal government spent $2.7 billion for Head Start services to 4.8 million children:

	Annual expenditures (millions)	Children enrolled (thousands)
1965	$103	580
1967	352	681
1969	302	635
1971	360	420
1973	400	379

Since 1969, Head Start has lacked a management information system, and this has allowed only the crudest guesstimates of per child costs. Some information on component costs and the variation of costs across programs is available from monitoring reports and grant applications (chart 11). An analysis of costs as budgeted in grant applications, although based on project proposals rather than actual expenditures, provides some ballpark estimates. On a national basis, the combined federal and nonfederal costs of part-day, full-year programs equaled $145 per month in 1972; and full-day programs averaged $176 (table 13). But real costs per child were higher. A sample study of summer 1972 Head Start programs revealed that the number of children actually enrolled was 3.5 percent less than the number funded and the absentee rate was 8.9 percent, which raised the actual average daily cost by 13 percent.[29] Absentee rates in full-year programs appear to have been higher than in summer programs. Studies of federally financed developmental day care centers indicated absentee rates averaging between one-third and one-fourth of enrollment, and children of a nonworking parent tended to have low attendance records.[30] Only about one-third of Head Start children had working mothers; and considering that the programs are conducted in the winter months when colds and bad weather are

TABLE 13. Estimated Head Start component costs, 1972.

	Full-year part-day	Full-year full-day
Cost/child/month	$145.00	$176.00
Cost/child/day	6.97	8.39
Percent distribution of component costs		
Total	100%	100%
Education	38	45
Transportation and facility	20	15
Parent and family (parent involvement and social services)	7	6
Health and psychological services	7	5
Nutrition	10	11
Career development and volunteers	1	1
Administration	18	16

Source: Pacific Training and Technical Assistance Corporation, "Data Analysis of Head Start Grant Applications," Contract No. HEW-OS-72-114, Office of Child Development, September 1972, pp. 69–71, 74–76.

more frequent, a 12 percent daily absentee rate for full-year programs would be quite conservative.

Teacher and administrative costs accounted for three of every five dollars expended. High staffing ratios and the fact that most teachers and staff were hired on a full-time basis even when the children attended part-day are major determinants of personnel costs. On the whole, Head Start salaries have been modest, but there has been considerable variation because local grantees had leeway in determining pay scales. A sample study of twelve southern states reported that in 1973 hourly wage rates for Head Start program directors ranged from $2.57 to $7.69, averaging $4.30. Teacher assistants' salaries ranged from $1.45 to $3.28 per hour, averaging $1.85.[31]

The 1972 amendments to the Higher Education Act brought Head Start and related preschool programs under the regulations of the Fair Labor Standards Act, making the federal minimum wage rates ($2.00 per hour in 1974, $2.10 in 1975, and $2.30 in 1976) applicable to all nonprofessional staff. In addition, all work exceeding forty hours per week had to be compensated by one and one-half the normal hourly rate. The new minimum required pay boosts to some teacher aides and other nonprofessional employees.

Programs in western and New England regions averaged the highest budgeted costs, and the southern states averaged the lowest. Contrary to general impressions, rural programs cost 10 percent more than urban pro-

CHART 11. Federal per child costs, 1968–1973.

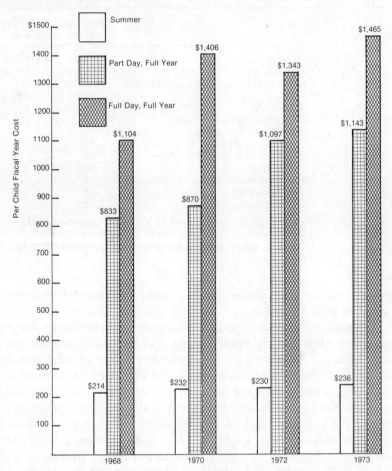

Source: U.S. Department of Health, Education, and Welfare, Office of Child Development, "Head Start Statistics FY 1968-1974," and "Head Start Costs, By Program, By Fiscal Year" (undated, unpublished data).

grams, and higher personnel costs, especially for teachers, accounted for almost the entire differential.[32] Apparently, Head Start was obliged to offer pay incentives to attract qualified staffs to rural settings.

Some economies of scale were realized when grantees ran very large projects, serving 300 or more children. However, the effects of program size on program quality were not indicated. An additional funding feature worth noting is that fourth quarter grants for each fiscal year carried significantly higher per child costs than each of the preceding three quarters. Given the uncertainties in Head Start funding, program operators apparently spent conservatively during the early part of the fiscal year. When contracts were reviewed during the final quarter, expenditures rose and earlier savings were expended. Since unobligated funds revert to the federal government, there was no incentive to maintain a surplus.

Costs per child varied dramatically, and projects with the highest performance records were not necessarily the most expensive ones. Monitoring reports of thirteen grantees operating full-year projects in 1972 found federal outlays ranging from $885 to $2,618 per child. The same projects were evaluated on the basis of their fulfillment of federal guidelines. Projects rated above the high performance benchmark reported per capita costs below the mean, while on two-thirds of the projects performing below the benchmark, per capita costs exceeded the mean.[33] Additional dollars do not dictate quality. Quality administrators and outside resources seem to be more salient factors.

Legislation mandating that handicapped children constitute at least 10 percent of Head Start enrollment apparently raised per capita costs. The handicapped, who required special education and related services, were reportedly excluded from many Head Start and other child development programs.[34] Preliminary Office of Child Development estimates predicted that services for handicapped children would cost two to three times more than those for nonhandicapped children and might, therefore, result in a 10 to 20 percent increase in total program costs for services to the same number of children.

ASSESSMENT—WHAT FUTURE
FOR HEAD START?

In 1974, at age nine, Head Start projects suffered from the practice of separating poor children from all other children, even if the programs were of the finest quality as measured by performance standards. If the public school system extends services to children aged three and four years, as recent trends suggest, poor children would attend public school facilities while Head Start funds might be concentrated on the coordination and delivery of supplementary services such as meals, health care, and parent education available through the community programs.

The concentration of resources in Head Start has been considerable. Nonetheless, funds were adequate to reach only a small proportion of eligible children. Some children have enrolled two or three years in succession; Head Start had invested several thousand dollars in their care and education before they reached the first grade. Since funding limitations have prevented all children from being served, the relative trade-offs of providing two years of experience to one child or one year of experience to two children might have been more carefully scrutinized.

Cost remains a constraint to designers of projects. Policymakers continually try to find the right combination of services—reaching children at younger ages, teaching mothers, providing food, delivering medical care—to produce measurable results. The IQ was dropped as an evaluative device because the validity of the measure was questioned, but critics charged that its use was discontinued because it demonstrated that the program's effects seem to fade, suggesting no returns on investment. Social competence provides a more elusive yardstick: it is harder to measure and more difficult to use in predicting long-range returns.

One Head Start goal has been effective parent education and parent involvement. Recent program performance standards and experimental program designs reemphasized the importance of the home and parents in directing the destinies of their children. Invariably, parental interest in and impact on children surpasses that of professional child development specialists. Also, the child development specialist remains a scarce commodity, whereas the supply of parents usually corresponds to the supply of children. The idea that families last longer than mutually supportive classmates again argues for home-based programs.

Teaching parents to take better care of their children may be cynically associated with Orwell's 1984 or, at best, considered an imposition of middle-class values. But a glance at Dr. Spock's book sales suggests an openness to child-rearing tips that transcends class lines. Head Start, along with schools in general, experienced clashes between professionals and parents over their respective roles in setting educational policy. In the case of Head Start, however, parents were encouraged to "meddle" in areas that professional educators had considered their exclusive turf. Tension between teachers and parents was not entirely absent in Head Start programs, and increasing professionalization of Head Start staffs may have widened the gap between parents and teachers.

The long-range impact of Head Start remains a matter of faith, although few would question the benefits enjoyed by the children who participated. Head Start enrollees enter the labor market a decade or more after their Head Start experience. Medical and dental care and adequate nutrition may mitigate future costs of health care, but even the most ardent advocates of cost-benefit calculations have found it far-fetched to try to measure the cost-effectiveness of nursery school in terms of later earning capacity, or even later school performance. Head Start provided services generally sought by parents for their children. History demonstrates that children can survive on less, but the American economy has adequate resources to spare poor children the discomfort that would otherwise be their lot. To argue that early childhood development programs are worthwhile even though their relationship to human capital formation is unproven does not mean that Head Start costs should be ignored. Perhaps an examination of alternative delivery systems is in order.

ALTERNATIVE COMPENSATORY STRATEGIES

In search of more effective compensatory programs, the federal Office of Child Development conducted demonstration models which departed from Head Start practices. One proposal was the substitution of the child's home for the center as the base for interaction, and the parent-as-teacher theme permeated home-based models. Parent-child centers concentrated on children under three years old on the premise that the damage is done by the time children enter Head Start and earlier intervention is necessary. Home Start concentrated on teaching parents to teach their children and attempted to make educational resources more available in the child's home. Other programs emphasized family well-being and acted as referral centers for other community services.

Existing public school systems are a general alternative to separate institutions providing compensatory services. Title I of the Elementary and Secondary Education Act provided federal funds to local school districts for special educational services to disadvantaged children, including those in kindergartens and nursery schools. As greater numbers of public school systems extend services down to age three, public schools may play increasing roles in providing compensatory programs for these children.

Parent-Child Centers. "Men may be equally born; but within its first month in the world, the baby will be adapting to a climate of experience that varies according to its family's social class."[35] Recognizing the deleterious effects of early deprivation and acting on the recommendations of the 1966 White House Task Force on Early Childhood, President Lyndon B. Johnson directed the Office of Economic Opportunity to establish a parent and child pilot program to help families with children under three years old living in acute poverty areas. Although designed as a research project in 1968, the actual implementation of the program was concerned with delivery of services, while research and evaluation took a back seat.

An annual $6 million federal contribution, plus the 20 percent local share, financed the operation of thirty-three centers. But the outlay per family was considerable. In 1972, each center served between 75 and 100 families, amounting to a total of 2,267 children under three years old and 6,033 older siblings. Adding the 20 percent local contribution, approximately $2,400 was invested in each family.[36]

Program objectives and eligibility criteria were similar to those of Head Start's, except that target children were younger than three years old. Also, the program placed stronger emphasis on parent education and family functioning. Services were extended to all family members on the premise that the family unit affects the development of the child.

Resources and services varied among centers, but included some day care services, counseling on health, nutrition, family planning, instruction on child-care techniques, and provision of homemaker services. In addition to direct delivery of services, centers advised clients about Medicaid, food stamps, and other welfare programs available to poor people.

A 1973 study attempted to assess the impacts of participation in the parent-child center program. Parents were divided into three groups: those who had participated less than one month, six to twenty months, and twenty months or more. In the absence of any "approved" child-rearing practice, the study faced the inherent difficulty of appraising presumed changes in behavior patterns. Acknowledging that quantifiable measurements were elusive, the study nonetheless concluded that the program changed few child-rearing practices of parents and that the length of participation in the program apparently made no difference. The level of involvement seemed to increase knowledge and use of community facilities only marginally. Long-term urban participants became better informed about the availability of recreational facilities, but no difference was noted for rural participants. Awareness and use of free legal services, housing authorities, employment offices, and job training programs were not conditional on parent-child center participation, nor were these factors associated with increased participation on community boards.[37]

Child Advocacy. Seven parent-child centers also added a child advocacy component paid for by an additional $100,000 grant to each center. Program goals included identification of unmet needs of low-income children under five years, identification of available community resources, and the formation of a comprehensive service delivery system. Child advocacy also aspired to heighten family awareness and utilization of community resources, and to encourage community organization efforts which could take over advocacy center functions in the future.

Assessment of first-year activities indicated that advocacy centers had performed outreach functions, including referrals to other agencies. The program was successful in filling some knowledge gaps about existing community services. But program planners' hopes that aided parents would take the initiative and form community self-help groups to carry on the work of advocacy centers did not materialize.[38] Poor people who want and need help are not necessarily equipped or inclined to carry out similar functions for others. Finding the means to cope with one's own problems does not necessarily motivate or equip people to tackle the problems of others. Also, the program had difficulty in maintaining staff, experiencing a 50 percent turnover among outreach workers during the first year. In order to prevent loss of in-service training benefits, advocacy centers had to forgo the hiring of indigenous staff and employ more experienced and committed staff.

Home Start. The Home Start demonstration project initiated during fiscal year 1972 presented an alternative vehicle for delivering Head Start services to the child's home that contrasted with the center-based approach. Home Start focused on "involving parents as the *major* means of helping the child." [39]

With a modest budget of $1.6 million in 1973, each of the sixteen projects served approximately eighty families at an average cost of $1,400 per family. The program hoped to demonstrate and evaluate alternatives to center-based comprehensive child development services, especially in areas where the center approach was not feasible. [40]

Home Start included all Head Start components and depended heavily on existing programs, but the program relied on parents for service delivery. For instance, nutritional services consisted of helping parents make the best uses of existing food resources and showing needy parents how to get additional assistance from ongoing community programs, instead of directly providing food for children. Home visitors introduced parents to clinics, Medicaid, and other needed services. [41] In isolated areas, home visitors and traveling practical nurses took children's health histories and arranged transportation to distant care facilities. However, the program could not fully make up for the dearth of health care services in rural poverty areas. Rather than concentrating on individual children, the program recognized that home life is the most potent influence on all young children. Needless to say, even if the diagnosis is correct, it does not follow that a few visits by a social worker would affect child-rearing practices.

The demonstration projects attempted to present alternatives to Head Start practices by encouraging grantees to adjust program formats. Instead of focusing on classroom services in the tradition of nursery school or kindergarten, home-based projects attempted to modify parent behavior, attitudes, and child-rearing practices. The projects presented further evidence of the inherent difficulties in inducing behavioral changes among adults. Programs may be popular with parents without changing child-rearing patterns. It is possible that giving the parents the cash equivalent expended for the services might have been a better alternative than the diverse services offered. The poor may need the services, but they certainly need the cash.

The School System As an Agent for Compensatory Education. The public school system offers an alternative to Head Start for delivering compensatory programs to nursery school and kindergarten children. The Elementary and Secondary Education Act funneled about $1.4 billion into local educational systems in 1973, of which 7 percent provided services to children not yet in the first grade. The act was amended in 1974, shifting the funding formula to favor children living in impoverished families. This will shift funds from states paying relatively high welfare benefits to poorer rural states.

The fact that public schools are general service institutions with strong traditions of local control presents both advantages and disadvantages to using them as the base for compensatory programs. Political and bureaucratic barriers inherent in established institutions and the difficulties involved in requiring schools to allocate funds to help children from poor homes argue against utilizing schools as a vehicle for compensatory education. But even rigid institutions can be reshaped. Community pressures bolstered by federal dollars may persuade public schools to place greater emphasis on the needs of the poor and to provide compensatory services to them. This assumes that special funds will be available on a sustained basis to support those activities.

Federal Leadership in Compensatory Education. The Elementary and Secondary Education Act of 1965 was the first major federal effort to assist public and private schools in educating children from poor homes. To allay fears of federal encroachment, federal control over curriculum and school policy was proscribed. But the target population for benefits was identified. The church-state conflict over which the Catholic hierarchy had successfully fought federal school aid bills was hurdled by incorporating "child benefit" and "shared services" concepts into the bill, making public and private schools eligible for federal funds to combat the educational disadvantages of poor children.

Special efforts on behalf of educationally deprived children, a group which included disproportionate numbers of minority children and children who had been short-changed when educational resources had been parceled out by local and state systems, required change in the orientation of schools, which had traditionally favored the best and the brightest. Acceptance of federal education funds required compliance with school integration orders, making further overt resistance to integration increasingly costly.

State educational agencies were given new responsibilities (or burdens, depending upon one's view) for approving plans submitted by local educational agencies and distributing funds allocated to the state. State school of-

TABLE 14. Title I obligations and beneficiaries, fiscal 1973.

Category	Number of disadvantaged children	Obligations (in millions)
TOTAL	6,667,000	$1,585.2
Part A		
Local education agencies	6,100,000	1,390.2
State education agencies		
Handicapped children	158,000	60.9
Neglected and delinquent children and youthful offenders	59,000	22.1
Migrant children	300,000	58.4
Indian children	50,000	15.4
Grants for state administration	——	17.1
Part B		
Special incentive grants	——	8.2
Part C		
Grants to urban and rural schools	——	28.1

Source: U.S. Congress, House, Hearings Before a Subcommittee of the Committee on Appropriations, *Departments of Labor and Health, Education, and Welfare Appropriations for 1974*, Part 2 (Washington: Government Printing Office, 1973), pp. 285–288.

ficials tended to favor traditional general aid as opposed to the categorical stipulations.[42] Even when state agencies were motivated to carry out the objectives of the Elementary and Secondary Education Act, they lacked the staff to implement the program. Added federal administration funds were frequently of little help because low state salaries prevented the hiring of needed talent.

Finally, the federal Office of Education has suffered from almost constant reorganization and shifts in priorities and top personnel since passage of ESEA. Congressman Daniel Flood's remark that "general councils come and go like Greyhound busses around here"[43] applied to the tenure of the Office of Education top officials. Continued juggling of chains of command precluded consistent policy direction from the federal establishment.

Components of ESEA. Title I-A of the Elementary and Secondary Education Act is the core of the compensatory effort. In 1973, 6.1 million children—almost three-fourths of all their eligible—were enrolled in 13,900 Title I school districts. A total of $1,390 million was divided among local educational agencies, adding approximately 229 dollars to the per pupil expenditure for disadvantaged children (table 14).[44]

Concentration on Young Children. The use of Title I funds to provide preprimary programs was encouraged. Out of $1.35 billion expended in the United States, $59.3 million assisted the education of 273,000 kindergartners and $37.7 million assisted 174,000 children in nursery school programs during fiscal year 1973. The proportion of funds spent on preprimary schools rose from 4.6 percent in 1969 to nearly 7 percent in 1973.

As the Coleman report suggested, the quality of education and the quantity of dollars are not necessarily directly related.[45] Successful compensatory strategies, particularly on the preschool level, are not artifacts of cost alone, since they deal with complex and interrelated problems.

The Title I mechanism for delivering compensatory programs at the preelementary level has some advantages over other strategies. The programs offer special services to disadvantaged children in an institutional setting that serves all the children in an area. Even if the school is not integrated because of residential patterns, the setting precludes the stigma of a segregated institution for the poor. Creating separate educational institutions for poor children perpetuates economic segregation. If an institution is identified primarily as a poverty program and charges a fee to nonpoor children, it is likely that services will be purchased elsewhere. On the other hand, public schools serving the general public can offer compensatory education by identifying children with special needs and offering them the services they need.

The primary problem associated with using the public school system to deliver compensatory programs is "dilution of services." This may occur in two ways. Funds may be spread too thinly to reach all eligible schools, or services may be shared with "nondisadvantaged" classmates. Recent increased emphasis on allocation of funds to schools with the highest concentrations of disadvantaged children countered the practice of too many schools receiving too few funds, but it ignored the needs of poor children enrolled in schools that are not funded. The dilution of services within a school presents an even more difficult dilemma. Offering the special services to disadvantaged children by separating them from their peers stigmatizes the beneficiaries. However, if Title I children receive special services in the general classroom setting, then classmates will share in the benefits, thus diluting the limited resources.

Some public schools have been charged with diversion of Title I funds for general purposes and insensitivity to the educational needs of the disadvantaged. There is a greater chance that programs will miss intended beneficiaries when delivered through general institutions. On the other hand, the Head Start program concentrated services on a needy clientele, but it accomplished this at a high cost of economic and racial segregation. Programs run by public schools suffer from some of the same problems because of residential patterns, but not by design. The third alternative is provision of services in the child's home through parent education programs. Conceptually, this approach is appealing because parents and home life are far more influential in shaping children's development than are schools. However, the initial results achieved from the demonstration projects leave little room for optimism about this strategy.

Expectations for Head Start and other compensatory strategies for preschoolers must be tempered by the current state of the art. Major gaps remain in understanding the maturation processes of children, and educators have not found the formula for successful early intervention. The increased resources add to the physical comfort and well-being of deprived children, but there is no guarantee that the extra funds will improve their educational careers.

CHAPTER EIGHT / TOWARD
A SINGLE SYSTEM

WORKING MOTHERS

The pattern of young mothers increasingly working outside the home is not likely to reverse in the foreseeable future. The high living standard which Americans have come to regard as "average" lies beyond the grasp of many single earners, requiring the additional earnings of wives. Married couples who (now) defer first births become used to living standards based on two incomes and feel "poor" if the birth of children curtails the wives' earning power. Keeping up with the Joneses and one's own expectations will keep mothers working.

Other factors contributing to women working outside the home are their higher educational achievements, their acquisition of more salable skills, and the breakdown of discriminatory barriers, all of which enable them to demand greater remuneration for their work. Increased earnings raise the opportunity costs of forgoing employment to care for children. Devoting full time to raising children becomes too expensive when a pay check is substantial.

As a byproduct of these reasons and others, American parents are favoring smaller families. The popularity of the two-child family is reinforced by the expense of raising children "properly." Larger families pose threats to economic status. Smaller family size combined with modern housework technology leads to more leisure time for wives—leisure time which is increasingly traded off for additional earnings. The recent popularity of Zero Population Growth is one manifestation of the provision of social sanction with a moral overtone to the preference for lower birth rates.

The recent weakening of marriage as an institution has made more children dependent upon their mothers for support. Divorce, desertion, and illegitimacy have swelled the ranks of single women with young children facing the options of work, welfare, or destitution. Many experience all three. Because of family disruption coupled with poverty, these women may have the greatest claims to society's assistance.

Finally, there have always been families in which the male head has earned low pay because of health, training, choice, or other factors. These men are married in disproportionate numbers to women who also have labor force handicaps. Over one and one-half million mothers of preschool-age children were married to men who earned less than $5,000 in 1972, and about two-fifths of these women worked.

The constantly rising number of employed mothers with young children, combined with the spread of support for the poor, has given rise to new arrangements to care for and educate the young before they reach the traditional school age.

THE STRUCTURE OF
CHILD CARE

Most work-related child care remains informal, unregulated, and low cost, provided mostly by family members or neighbors. In addition to low cost, the traditional system allows maximum flexibility in making arrangements which meet parents' needs. But easy access to acceptable low-cost arrangements is not always available to those most in need, and the cost of care is not necessarily commensurate with ability to pay. Some parents have no choice but to accept arrangements they consider inadequate, and to pay for them.

The increasing numbers of mothers requiring child care have outstripped the supply of informal arrangements which satisfy parents. The public policy issue is the choice of preferred alternatives that would expand needed facilities. A voucher system has been favored by some, but these recommendations are based more on ideology than on empirical evidence that such a program would best satisfy child-care and education needs. The additional vouchers may not insure that adequate and convenient child-care options can be bought or that services would be offered on a nondiscriminatory basis. Abuses of custodial care have led to demands for establishing standards and monitoring child-care arrangements. Maintaining high quality standards is expensive, and close monitoring inflates costs without necessarily improving services. Monitoring may prevent flagrant abuses, but its effectiveness is doubtful, especially since it compromises the rights of parents to decide how they will care for their children.

Making quality care a public rather than a private responsibility is an alternative to exhortation and monitoring. In a society where the government has been assuming an increasing role in providing services to the citizenry, public provision for child care has considerable appeal. Cost has been a major obstacle, and demonstration projects indicate that costs are not necessarily correlated with quality of care provided or measurable results.

In the last decade, society broadened its role in direct provision of child care, but most strategies favored children's educational needs, while few programs focused on work-related child-care needs. In addition to general education programs and the provision of child care for mothers on welfare, special compensatory efforts were mounted to help poor children. Head Start has undoubtedly enhanced the health and well-being of enrolled children. But nine years of experience and evaluation offer little to support the view that one adult to four children is a more effective ratio than one to fifteen in promoting cognitive achievement, health, or welfare of children. Given that school for younger children will expand in the upcoming years, perhaps the educational needs of poor children should be met by providing additional special services to children attending general school programs rather than by maintaining independent systems, even if the latter enjoy higher funding levels. The best solution may be to somehow combine informal, low-cost care with formal public educational programs for young children, thus satisfying educational and work-related needs.

PAYING FOR CHILD CARE

Federal, state, and local tax dollars plus parental outlays make child-care and educational services for young children a $6 billion industry that is rapidly growing. But the incidence of cost and of government benefits remain unevenly distributed, even among families with comparable claims for assistance. The high cost of center care limits its expansion, even assuming that mothers would prefer this type of care. Limiting eligibility to the poor and near poor tends to further segregate poor children. Moreover, the high costs generate resentment against the segregated system.

Options for public subsidy of child care are available. Unutilized excess capacity in schools resulting from a declining birth rate will motivate school systems to assume an increasing role in caring for children now considered "preschool" age. Any institution abhors a vacuum and resists a decline in its role. Since educational provisions for young adults beyond secondary school are preempted by junior and community colleges, public schools have nowhere to turn but down the age spectrum. Schools are reluctant, however, to assume responsibility of caring for children of working mothers, and many parents may not favor such an arrangement. But expansion of public education for three- and four-year olds will lighten direct parental outlays for child care as it did for older children.

Attention has been turned to utilizing the tax system as a means of helping families to defray the cost of child care. Initially enacted to provide relief to low-income single mothers, the income tax law was modified in 1971 to expand assistance to most families with working mothers who incur child-care expenses. But tax breaks only assist those with tax liabilities and are of little use to the poor and near poor.

In assessing who should pay for child care, the relative benefits and burdens of child-care benefits must be considered. The poor have the most obvious need for the additional income provided by the mother's earnings. Arguments for subsidizing the income and defraying work expenses of middle-income mothers may be based more on political clout than on equity. But if government intervenes to regulate the quality of care, limiting parents' options to arrangements with much higher costs than those for which they had been paying, then society would be obligated to pay some of the additional costs.

If universal child care were provided on the same basis as public education, added expenses would be reflected in additional taxes, reduction of other government programs, or deficit financing whose costs would ultimately be spread among all taxpayers. Benefits conditioned on employment will increase the opportunity costs of mothers not working and will have the net effect of encouraging more mothers to work outside their homes. If greater numbers of mothers married to high-earning men take jobs, there is likely to be a widening gap between the incomes of those families and the incomes of the working poor and female-headed families.

SCOPE AND GOALS

The expansion of child-care facilities during the past decade has not been accompanied by any consensus about the proper role and future direction for such facilities. Conflicts persist, not only over the goals but also over how to structure the system to achieve quality care and who should pay the tab. The review of current child-care practices reveals fragmented, incomplete, and overlapping structures for education and care of preschool children. Removing obstacles to employment of mothers, defraying work expenses, educating preschool-age children to prepare them for primary school, or compensating children who live in poverty are all approaches that reflect the many needs or diverse wants of different social groups. The ability of child-care systems to satisfy the multiple goals varies. Government outlays cover education and child-care costs for an increasing number of children, but the distribution of benefits has been uneven, even among families with comparable claims for assistance. The search for quality has been elusive and difficult to assess.

Agreement on a goal may be based on different assumptions of need. Providing child care in order to remove work obstacles may be welcomed by some but perceived as coercive by others. Child care may satisfy the practical needs of married and single parents who need to work for financial reasons. Availability of child care may also be viewed as a precondition for requiring welfare mothers to work or as a means of assisting mothers in exercising their choice to seek gainful employment.

While government programs, either through subsidies or direct services, have been expanding, child-care facilities are still far from universal. The expense entailed in universal care is only one obstacle to government assumption of broader responsibility. There is also no agreement on the form in which government aid should be given and what level of government should assume the responsibility for preschool education. As the federal government is assuming an increasing share of elementary and secondary school costs, some advocate federal funding to speed up expansion of preschool facilities.

Society has experimented with free or subsidized care, targeting on the poor and near poor, either to induce mothers to work or because this group's claims on governmental assistance have had the greatest appeal. Provision of free child care has done little, however, to encourage employment of poor mothers. Alternative income support through the welfare system has frequently proven to be preferable to the meager self-support within the reach of poor women. Given discriminatory practices in the labor market, the limited jobs skills, and other handicaps of welfare mothers, child care is not enough to guarantee gainful and sustained employment. Moreover, the hope of some that inducing welfare mothers to work would reduce public assistance rolls has not materialized because the cost of providing child care and other needed services to marginal workers often exceeds the cost of direct support. Most women who do not work because of child "problems" prefer to care for their own children and do not seek employment. The offering of child care has apparently induced few nonworkers into the labor force.

The provision of nursery or kindergarten facilities in the school system providing part-day care and education during school hours may be adequate for many mothers, but these programs are not designed to enable mothers to work. To maintain separate facilities for children of working mothers tends to segregate these children, especially if eligibility for enrollment is based on poverty. To help working mothers, child care that would supplement expanded school programs rather than compete with them is a preferred alternative to segregated systems. The added school facilities would be open to all children in keeping with traditional practice of serving children from all classes. Federal guidelines and monitoring may be required to assure that the needs of children from low-income homes are not ignored in the universal system.

NOTES

CHAPTER TWO/WORKING MOTHERS

1. Howard Hayghe, "Marital and Family Characteristics of the Labor Force in March 1973," U.S. Bureau of Labor Statistics, Special Labor Force Report No. 164, p. 26.

2. Elizabeth Waldman and Kathryn R. Gover, "Marital and Family Characteristics of the Labor Force," *Monthly Labor Review,* April 1972, p. 8.

3. Institute for Research on Poverty and Mathematica, *Summary Report: The New Jersey Graduated Work Incentive Program* (Washington: U.S. Department of Health, Education, and Welfare, December 1973).

4. Sookim Kim, Roger D. Roderick, John R. Shea, *Dual Careers: A Longitudinal Study of Labor Market Experience of Women,* Vol. II (Columbus, Ohio: Ohio State University Center for Human Resource Research, 1973), pp. 24, 71.

5. U.S. Department of Labor, Bureau of Labor Statistics, Summary/Special Labor Force Report, "Children of Working Mothers, March 1973," September 1973, Table 2.

6. Howard Hayghe, "Marital and Family Characteristics of the Labor Force, March 1973," U.S. Bureau of Labor Statistics, Special Labor Force Report No. 164, p. 20.

7. Herbert S. Parnes, John R. Shea, Ruth S. Spitz, Frederick A. Zeller, and Associates, *Dual Careers: A Longitudinal Study of Labor Market Experience of Women,* Vol. I (Washington: Government Printing Office, 1970), p. 73.

8. U.S. Bureau of the Census, "Marital Status and Living Arrangements: March 1973," Series P-20, No. 255, November 1973, Tables C and D.

9. U.S. Bureau of the Census, "Birth Expectations of American Wives: June 1973," Series P-20, No. 254, October 1973, Table 2.

10. Phillips Cutright and John Scanzoni, "Income Supplements and the American Family," U.S. Congress, Joint Economic Committee, *Studies in Public Welfare,* No. 12, Part 1 (Washington: Government Printing Office, 1973), p. 67.

11. Heather L. Ross, "Poverty: Women and Children Last" (Washington: The Urban Institute), Working Paper 971-08-02, December 5, 1973, pp. 5–6.

12. U.S. Department of Labor, Bureau of Labor Statistics, *Earnings and Employment,* Vol. 19, No. 7, January 1973, p. 164.

13. Robert L. Stein, "Reasons for Nonparticipation in the Labor Force," *Monthly Labor Review,* July 1967, pp. 23–26.

14. W. Joseph Heffernan, "Variations in Negative Tax Rates in Current Public Assistance Programs: An Example of Administrative Discretion," *Journal of Human Resources,* Supplement 1973, pp. 65–66.

15. Sar A. Levitan, Martin Rein, and David Marwick, *Work and Welfare Go Together* (Baltimore: Johns Hopkins Press, 1972), p. 16.

16. *Manpower Report of the President, 1974* (Washington: Government Printing Office, 1974), Table A-3; and U.S. Department of Health, Education, and Welfare, AFDC surveys for 1961, 1967, 1969, 1971, and 1973.

17. Vee Burke and Alair A. Townsend, "Public Welfare and Work Incentives: Theory and Practice," U.S. Congress, Joint Economic Committee, *Studies in Public Welfare,* Paper No. 14 (Washington: Government Printing Office, 1974), p. 3.

CHAPTER THREE/HOW DO WORKING MOTHERS CARE FOR THEIR CHILDREN?

1. Henry C. Lajewski, *Child Care Arrangements of Full-Time Working Mothers,* Publication No. 378 (Washington: Government Printing Offices, 1959), p. 15; John R. Shea, Roger D. Roderick, Frederick A. Zeller, Andrew I. Kohen, and Associates, *Years for Decision: A Longitudinal Study of the Educational and Labor Market Experience of Young Women,* Vol. 1 (Columbus, Ohio: Ohio State University Center for Human Resource Research, 1971), p. 135; and Seth Low and Pearl G. Spindler, *Child Care Arrangements of Working Mothers in the United States* (Washington: Government Printing Office, 1968), p. 71.

2. Shea *et al., Years for Decision,* Vol. 1, p. 138.

3. Low and Spindler, *Child Care Arrangements of Working Mothers in the United States,* p. 79.

4. U.S. Congress, Senate Committee on Finance, *Child Care: Data and Materials* (Washington: Government Printing Office, 1974), pp. 104–119.

5. Howard Schneider, *Final Report: Part VI, Public Opinion Toward Day Care* (Minneapolis, Minn.: Institute for Interdisciplinary Studies, 1971), pp. 16, 17.

6. Florence A. Ruderman, *Child Care and Working Mothers: A Study of Arrangements Made for Daytime Care for Children* (New York: Child Welfare League, 1968), p. 298.

7. *Ibid.*, p. 327.

8. Westinghouse Learning Corporation and Westat Research, *Day Care Survey 1970—Summary Report and Basic Analysis* (Rockville, Md.: Westinghouse Learning Corporation and Westat Research, 1971), p. 163.

9. Richard B. Zamoff and Jerolyn R. Lyle, *Assessment of Day Care Services and Needs at the Community Level: Mt. Pleasant* (Washington: The Urban Institute, 1971), pp. 20 and 30.

10. Jack Ditmore and W. R. Prosser, *A Study of Day Care's Effect on the Labor Force Participation of Low Income Mothers*, Office of Economic Opportunity, Office of Planning, Research and Evaluation, June 1973, p. 34.

11. Camil Associates, Inc., *Evolution of Supportive Services Provided for Participants of Manpower Programs,* U.S. Department of Labor Contract No. 43-1-008-42 (Philadelphia: Camil Associates, Inc., 1972), p. 6.

12. State of Vermont Family Assistance Planning Unit and Mathmatica, Inc., *Vermont Family Assistance Plan,* as cited in Vivian Lewis, "Day Care: Needs, Costs, Benefits, Alternatives," U.S. Congress, Joint Economic Committee, *Studiesin Public Welfare*, Paper No. 7 (Washington: Government Printing Office, 1973), p. 116.

13. General Accounting Office, *Some Problems in Contracting for Federally Assisted Child Care Services*, B-164031(3) (Washington: General Accounting Office, June 13, 1973), pp. 16–17, 28.

14. Ditmore and Prosser, *A Study of Day Care's Effect on the Labor Force Participation of Low Income Mothers,* p. 18.

15. *Ibid.*, Appendix A.

16. Robert L. Stein, "Reasons for Nonparticipation in the Labor Force," *Monthly Labor Review,* July 1967, p. 24.

17. Harvey J. Helaski, "Unutilized Manpower in Poverty Areas of Six U.S. Cities," *Monthly Labor Review,* December 1971 (reprint), pp. 1–63.

18. Herbert S. Parnes, John R. Shea, Ruth S. Spitz, Frederick A. Zeller, and Associates, *Dual Careers: A Longitudinal Study of Labor Market Experience of Women,* Vol. I (Washington: Government Printing Office, 1970), p. 83.

19. John R. Shea and Jack A. Meyer, *Potential Recipients of Family Assistance Payments: Characteristics and Labor Market Behavior* (Columbus, Ohio: Ohio State University Center for Human Resource Research, 1972), p. 82.

20. Susan Stein, "The Company Cares for Children," in *Child Care: Who Cares?: Foreign and Domestic Infant and Early Childhood Development Policies,* ed. Pamela Roby (New York: Basic Books, 1973), p. 245.

21. *Ibid.*, p. 259.

22. William Prosser, Foreword to *Evaluation of the Office of Economic Opportunity Child Development Center* (Rockville, Md.: Westat, Inc., 1972), pp. xi-xxvi.

23. Claudia Levy, "Few Attend C & P Day Care Center," *Washington Post,* August 5, 1973.

24. Vivian Lewis, "Day Care: Needs, Costs, Benefits, Alternatives," U.S. Congress, Joint Economic Committee, *Studies in Public Welfare,* No. 7, (Washington: Government Printing Office, 1973), p. 146.

25. Donald G. Ogilvie, *Employer-Subsidized Child Care* (Washington: Inner City Fund, 1973), p. 56.

26. *Gwen Morgan of KLH as quoted by Claudia Levy, "Few Attend C & P's Day Care Center," Washington Post,* August 5, 1973.

27. Ogilvie, *Employer-Subsidized Child Care,* pp. 85, 92.

CHAPTER FOUR/CHILD CARE—WHO PAYS, HOW MUCH, AND FOR WHAT?

1. Westinghouse Learning Corporation and Westat Research, *Day Care Survey 1970—Summary Report and Basic Analysis* (Rockville, Md.: Westinghouse Learning Corporation and Westat Research, 1971), p. 89.
2. Lynn C. Thompson, *A Study in Child Care 1970-71, Vol. III: Costs and Quality Issues for Operators* (Cambridge, Mass.: Abt Associates, 1971), Table IV.
3. Council for Community Services in Metropolitan Chicago, *Findings: Day Care Cost Analysis Project* (Chicago: The Council, 1972), p. 29.
4. *Ibid.*, p. 16.
5. U.S. Congress, Senate Committee on Finance, *Child Care: Data and Materials* (Washington: Government Printing Office, 1971), p. 11.
6. Thompson, *A Study in Child Care 1970-71, Vol. III,* Table IV.
7. W. R. Prosser, "Day Care in the Seventies—Some Thoughts," Office of Economic Opportunity Pamphlet 3250-5, May 1972, p. 8.
8. U.S. Department of Health, Education, and Welfare, "Social Services Under Title IV, Part A of the Social Security Act: Child Care, Fiscal Year 1972 and 1973," February 6, 1973 (unpublished table).
9. See: Department of Health, Education, and Welfare, Community Services Administration, "WIN Quarterly Report," CSA-9, and NCSS Report E-4, "Child Care Arrangements of AFDC Recipients Under the Work Incentive Program," September 31, 1972, December 31, 1972, March 31, 1973, and June 30, 1973.
10. AVCO Corporation, "A Demonstration Child Care Review System, Final Report," Contract HEW, SRS 71-48, Attachment: Vol. 1 (Washington: AVCO International Services Division, 1973).
11. *Ibid.*, Tables S-B, T-B, TB-IS, "The Quality of Care and Teaching."
12. *Ibid.*, Table S-C, T-C.
13. Westinghouse Learning Corporation and Westat Research, *Day Care Survey 1970—Summary Report and Basic Analysis,* p. 163.
14. John R. Shea, Roger D. Roderick, Frederick A. Zeller, Andrew I. Kohen, and Associates, *Years for Decision: A Longitudinal Study of the Educational and Labor Market Experience of Young Women,* Vol. I (Columbus, Ohio: Ohio State University Center for Human Resource Research, 1971), p. 134.
15. W. Vance Grant and C. George Lind, *Digest of Educational Statistics: 1973 Edition* (Washington: Government Printing Office, 1974), p. 65.

CHAPTER FIVE/BEYOND MERE CARE

1. Ilse Forest, *Preschool Education: A Historical and Critical Study* (New York: The Macmillan Company, 1927), p. 170.
2. Josephine C. Foster and Neith E. Headley, *Education in the Kindergarten* (New York: American Book Company, 1943), p. 16.
3. The White House Conference of Child Health and Protection, *Nursery Education: A Survey of Day Nurseries, Nursery Schools, Private Kindergartens in the United States* (New York: The Century Company, 1931), p. 11.
4. Gordon E. Hurd, *Preprimary Enrollment Trends of Children Under Six: 1964-1968* (Washington: Government Printing Office, 1970), pp. 26-28.
5. Joseph Froomkin, J. R. Endriss, and Robert W. Stump, *Population, Enrollment, and Costs of Public Elementary and Secondary Education 1975-76 and 1980-81: A Report to the President's Commission on School Finance* (Washington: The President's Commission on School Finance, 1971), pp. 7, 88.
6. Linda A. Barker, *Preprimary Enrollment: October 1973,* DHEW Publication No. (OE) 73-11411 (Washington: Government Printing Office, 1973), p. 27.
7. Kenneth A. Simon and W. Vance Grant, *Digest of Educational Statistics: 1972 Edition* (Washington: Government Printing Office, 1973), p. 27.
8. U.S. Bureau of the Census, "Nursery School and Kindergarten Enrollment, October 1973," Series P-20, No. 268, August 1974, Table 2.

9. U.S. Department of Health, Education, and Welfare, *Monthly Vital Statistics Report*, January 30, 1970 and February 1974.

10. W. Vance Grant and C. George Lind, *Digest of Educational Statistics: 1973 Edition* (Washington: Government Printing Office, 1974), p. 31.

11. Gilbert R. Austin, "Differences in Early Childhood Education Practice and Policy: The Example of France and Sweden," in *Education Year Book 1974-75* (New York: Macmillan and Free Press, 1975).

12. Gilbert R. Austin and T. Neville Postlethwaite, "Cognitive Results Based on Different Ages of Entry to School: A Comparative Study," *Journal of Educational Psychology*, December 1974.

13. Westinghouse Learning Corporation and Westat Research, *Day Care Survey 1970—Summary Report and Basic Analysis* (Rockville, Md.: Westinghouse Learning Corporation and Westat Research, 1971), pp. 16, 63.

14. Federal Interagency Day Care Requirements, Code of Federal Regulations, Title 45, Subtitle A, Part 71.

15. U.S. Department of Health, Education, and Welfare, "Children Served by Public Welfare Agencies and Institutions," NCSS Report E-9 (3/71), April 27, 1973, Table 13.

16. Gilbert Y. Steiner, *The State of Welfare* (Washington: The Brookings Institution, 1971), p. 61.

17. Westinghouse Learning Corporation and Westat Research, *Day Care Survey 1970—Summary Report and Basic Analysis*, p. 42.

18. Mary Dublin Keyserling, *Windows on Day Care: A Report Based on Findings of the National Council of Jewish Women* (New York: National Council of Jewish Women, 1972), p. 82.

19. Westinghouse Learning Corporation and Westat Research, *Day Care Survey 1970—Summary Report and Basic Analysis*, p. 34.

20. Keyserling, *Windows on Day Care*, pp. 65, 86.

21. E. Belle Evans, Beth Scub, and Marlene Weinstein, *Day Care: How to Plan, Develop, and Operate a Day Care Center* (Boston: Beacon Press, 1971), pp. 258, 260, 262, 264.

22. Westinghouse Learning Corporation and Westat Research, *Day Care Survey 1970—Summary Report and Basic Analysis*, p. 17.

23. Keyserling, *Windows on Day Care*, pp. 89-90.

24. Christopher S. Jencks, "The Coleman Report and the Conventional Wisdom," in *On Equality of Educational Opportunity*, ed. Frederick Mosteller and Daniel P. Moynihan (New York: Vintage Books, 1972), p. 92.

25. Marshall S. Smith, "Equality of Educational Opportunity: Basic Findings Reconsidered," in *On Equality of Educational Opportunity*, p. 259.

26. For a summary of criticisms of the *Equality of Educational Opportunity* Report and Jensen's study, see Allan C. Ornstein, "Recent Historical Perspectives for Educating the Disadvantaged," in *Educating the Disadvantaged: 1970-1971*, ed. Russell E. Doll and Maxine Hawkins (New York: AMS Press, 1971), pp. 153-160.

27. Arthur R. Jensen, "How Much Can We Boost IQ and Scholastic Achievement?" *Harvard Educational Review*, January 1969, p. 81.

28. Harold M. Skeels, "Adult Status of Children with Contrasting Early Life Experiences: A Follow-up Study," in *Child Development and Behavior*, ed. Freda Rebelsky and Lynn Dorman (New York: Alfred A. Knopf, 1970), p. 207.

29. Robert D. Hess and Virginia C. Shipman, "Early Experience and the Socialization of Cognitive Modes in Children," in *Child Development and Behavior*, pp. 312, 322.

30. J. McVicker Hunt, "The Role of Experience in the Development of Competence," in *Human Intelligence*, ed. J. McVicker Hunt (New Brunswick, N.J.: Transaction Books, 1972), p. 49; *idem*, "The Implications of Changing Ideas on How Children Develop Intellectually," in *Child Development and Behavior*, pp. 306-308; and Marion Blank and Frances Solomon, "A Tutorial Language Program to Develop Abstract Thinking in Socially Disadvantaged Preschool Children," in *Child Development and Behavior*, pp. 376, 382.

31. Ray C. Rest, "The Self Fulfilling Prophecy in Ghetto Education," in *Human Intelligence*, pp. 128-129, 142, 143.

32. Estelle Fuchs, "How Teachers Learn to Help Children Fail," in *Human Intelligence*, pp. 117, 118.

33. Allan C. Ornstein, "Recent Historical Perspectives for Educating the Disadvantaged," in *Educating the Disadvantaged: 1970–1971*, pp. 156–158.

34. Stephen S. Baratz and Joan C. Baratz, "Early Childhood Intervention: The Social Science Base of Institutionalized Racism," in *Educating the Disadvantaged: School Year 1969/1970*, ed. Allan C. Ornstein, Russell C. Doll, Nancy L. Arnez, Maxine Hawkins (New York: AMS Press, 1971), p. 96.

35. Susan H. Houston, "A Reexamination of Some Assumptions About the Language of the Disadvantaged Child," in *Educating the Disadvantaged: 1970–1971*, pp. 263, 265, 269, 272.

36. Lorene C. Quay, "Language Dialect, Reinforcement, and Intelligence Test Performance of Negro Children," in *Educating the Disadvantaged: 1970–1971*, pp. 84–85.

37. H. J. Eysnck, "Race, Intelligence, Education and IQ," *Intellectual Digest*, July 1972, p. 34.

CHAPTER SIX/THE FEDERAL CHILD-CARE DOLLAR

1. U.S. Congress, Senate Committee on Finance, *Child Care: Data and Materials* (Washington: Government Printing Office, 1971), p. 60.

2. U.S. Congress, Staff of the Joint Committee on Internal Revenue Taxation, *General Explanation of the Revenue Act of 1971* (Washington: Government Printing Office, 1972), p. 58.

3. U.S. Congress, Senate, Committee on Finance, *Child Care: Data and Materials* (Washington: Government Printing Office, 1974), pp. 102–103.

4. U.S. Congress, Senate Committee on Labor and Public Welfare, *Head Start, Child Development Legislation, 1972* (Washington: Government Printing Office, 1972), pp. 475, 476.

5. U.S. Congress, House Committee on Ways and Means, "Tax Reform Legislation, Tentative Decision for Drafting Purposes Only," Release No. 6, May 20, 1974.

6. U.S. Congress, Joint Economic Committee, *Open-Ended Federal Matching of State Social Services Expenditure Authorized Under the Public Assistance Titles of the Social Security Act* (Washington: Government Printing Office, 1972), p. 6.

7. "Federalism Report/Revenue Sharing Bill Authorizes Sweeping Innovations in Federal Aid System," *National Journal*, October 7, 1972, p. 1564.

8. Touche Ross & Co., *Cost Analyses of Social Services, Fiscal Year 1972*, U.S. Department of Health, Education and Welfare, February 2, 1973, p. 34.

9. U.S. Department of Health, Education and Welfare, "Report on Audit of Child Care Services Under Title IV of the Social Security Act, State of Washington," Audit Control No. 40002-10, February 15, 1974, p. 35.

10. U.S. Department of Health, Education, and Welfare, "Report on Review of Day Care Programs Administered by the Department of Public Welfare," State of Texas, Audit Control No. 06-30031, February 28, 1973, pp. 17, 20.

11. Comptroller General of the United States, *Some Problems in Contracting for Federally Assisted Child Care Services*, B-164031(3), June 13, 1973, pp. 26–27.

12. U.S. Department of Health, Education and Welfare, "Report on Review of Child Care Services Purchased by the Department of Social Welfare through Interagency Agreements with the Department of Education—Title IV—Part A," State of California, Audit Control No. 40016-09, February 28, 1974, p. 7.

13. U.S. Department of Health, Education, and Welfare, "Report on Audit of Child Care Services Under Title IV of the Social Security Act, State of Washington," Audit Control No. 40002-10, February 15, 1974, pp. 6–8; "Report on Review of Child Care Services—State of New Jersey," Audit Control No. 40007-02, June 30, 1972, pp. 6–7; "Review of Child Care Programs as Administered by the Commonwealth of Massachusetts," Audit Control No. 40018-01, November, 1973, p. 3; Comptroller General of the United States, *Some Problems in Contracting for Federally Assisted Child Care Services*, B-164031(3), June 13, 1973, pp. 16–17.

14. "Major Change in WIN Requires Registration of Welfare Applicants," *Manpower Information Service*, May 22, 1974, p. 369.

15. U.S. Department of Labor, "Women in Apprenticeship—Why Not? " Manpower Research Monograph No. 33 (Washington: Government Printing Office, 1974), p. 15.

16. Social Welfare Regional Research Institute, *Final Report: WIN II Initial Impact Study,* SRS Grant No. 10-P-56104/1-01, December 1972, pp. v–10.

17. Camil Associates, Inc., *Evaluation of Supportive Services Provided for Participants of Manpower Programs,* U.S. Department of Labor, Contract No. 43-1-008-42 (Philadelphia: Camil Associates, Inc., 1972), pp. v–10.

18. Camil Associates, Inc., *Final Report: Welfare Dependency, Termination and Employment: An AFDC Review* (Philadelphia: Camil Associates, Inc., October 21, 1972), p. 47.

19. U.S. Congress, House Committee on Appropriations, *Departments of Labor and Health, Education, and Welfare Appropriations for 1974,* Part 5 (Washington: Government Printing Office, 1973), p. 407.

20. Social Welfare Regional Research Institute, *Final Report: Win II Initial Impact Study,* SRS, Grant No. 10-P-56104/1-01, December 1972, pp. 11–12.

CHAPTER SEVEN/HEAD START—FIGHTING POVERTY WITH EARLY EDUCATION

1. Sar A. Levitan, *The Great Society's Poor Law* (Baltimore: Johns Hopkins Press, 1969), pp. 133–163.

2. Richard M. Nixon, "Poverty Message," February 19, 1969, *CQ Almanac 1969* (Washington: Congressional Quarterly, 1970), p. 33-A.

3. U.S. Department of Health, Education, and Welfare, Office of Child Development, *Project Head Start 1969–1970: A Descriptive Report of Programs and Participants* (Washington: Office of Child Development, 1972), p. 164.

4. Dr. Max Wolff, quoted in: U.S. Congress, Hearings before the Senate Subcommittee on Employment, Manpower, and Poverty of the Committee on Labor and Public Welfare, *Examination of the War on Poverty,* Part 8 (Washington: Government Printing Office, 1967), p. 2451.

5. U.S. Department of Health, Education, and Welfare, Office of Child Development, "Using Head Start Funds to Provide Full Day Services," Notice N-30-336-1-00, August 21, 1972.

6. *Congressional Record* (daily edition), H10487-10488, December 3, 1973.

7. "OEO, Child Care Program: Veto Sustained in the Senate," *CQ Almanac: 1971* (Washington: Congressional Quarterly, 1971), p. 504.

8. U.S. Department of Health, Education, and Welfare, Project Head Start, *Speech, Language, and Hearing Program: A Guide for Head Start Personnel,* DHEW Publication No. (OCD) 73-1025 (Washington: Government Printing Office, 1973), p. 35.

9. U.S. Department of Health, Education, and Welfare, *The Effectiveness of Compensatory Education: Summary and Review* (Washington: Department of Health, Education, and Welfare, 1972), pp. 111–112.

10. Walter Williams and John W. Evans, "The Politics of Evaluation: The Case of Head Start," *The Annals,* September 1969, pp. 126–128.

11. U.S. Department of Health, Education, and Welfare, *The Effectiveness of Compensatory Education,* pp. 114–115.

12. Development Associates, *Final Quarterly Profile Analysis Report,* Contract No. HEW-OS-72-52 (Washington: Development Associates, 1972), pp. 7–8.

13. U.S. Department of Health, Education, and Welfare, Office of Child Development, *Project Head Start 1969–1970,* p. 125.

14. Marion S. Stearns, *Report on Preschool Programs: The Effects of Preschool Programs on Disadvantaged Children and Their Families* (Washington: Government Printing Office, 1971), p. 82.

15. Development Associates, *Final Quarterly Profile Analysis Report,* pp. 5–6.

16. U.S. Department of Health, Education, and Welfare, Office of Child Development, *Project Head Start 1968: The Development of a Program* (Washington: Office of Child Development, 1970), p. 12.

17. U.S. Department of Health, Education, and Welfare, Project Head Start, *Health*

Services: A Guide for Project Directors and Health Personnel, DHEW Publication No. (OCD) 724 (Washington: Government Printing Office, 1971), pp. 11–12.

18. U.S. Department of Health, Education and Welfare, Office of Child Development, "Announcement for Head Start Collaboration with Medicaid Early and Periodic Screening, Diagnosis, and Treatment Program," December 18, 1973.

19. Kirshner Associates, Inc., *A National Survey of the Impacts of Head Start Centers on Community Institutions: Summary Report* (Washington: Department of Health, Education, and Welfare, 1970), p. 6.

20. U.S. Department of Health, Education, and Welfare, Office of Child Development, *Project Head Start 1969–1970,* pp.97–99.

21. *Ibid.,* pp. 87–89.

22. Leona M. Vogt *et al., Health Start: Summary of the Evaluation of the Second Year Program,* Urban Institute Grant Report 964-5 (Washington: The Urban Institute, 1973), p. 23.

23. Development Associates, *Final Quarterly Profile Analysis Report,* p. 14.

24. U.S. Department of Health, Education, and Welfare, *Project Head Start 1969–1970,* pp. 97–98.

25. *Ibid.,* p. 31.

26. Stearns, *Report on Preschool Programs,* p. 101.

27. Development Associates, *Final Quarterly Profile Analysis Report,* pp. 22, 31.

28. U.S. Department of Health, Education, and Welfare, Office of Child Development, *The CDA Program: The Child Development Associate,* DHEW Publication No. (OCD) 73-1065 (Washington: Office of Child Development, 1973), p. 18.

29. U.S. Department of Health, Education, and Welfare, Office of Child Development, "Summary of Summer Head Start Program Monitoring, Summer 1972" (unpublished, no date).

30. General Accounting Office, *Some Problems in Contracting for Federally Assisted Child Care Services,* B-164031(3), June 13, 1973, p. 27.

31. Roy Littlejohn Associates, *The Impact of the Fair Labor Standards Act on the Head Start Program in HEW Region IV and Region VI,* Contract No. SBC-2-0-8(a) 73 C 247 (Washington: Roy Littlejohn Associates, 1973), pp. 40, 42, 47.

32. Pacific Training and Technical Assistance Corporation, "Data Analysis of Head Start Grant Application," Contract No. HEW-OS-72-114, Office of Child Development, September 1972 (mimeo.), pp. 49–51.

33. Development Associates, *Final Quarterly Profile Analysis Report* (Washington: Development Associates, 1972), p. 20.

34. U.S. Congress, Senate Subcommittee on Children and Youth and the Subcommittee on Employment, Manpower, and Poverty of the Committee on Labor and Public Welfare, *Head Start, Child Development Legislation, 1972* (Washington: Government Printing Office, 1972), p. 612.

35. John and Elizabeth Newson, *Infant Care in an Urban Community* (New York: International Universities Press, 1963), p. 229.

36. U.S. Department of Health, Education, and Welfare, Office of Child Development, "Project Head Start Statistical Fact Sheet, Fiscal Year 1972."

37. Monica B. Holmes, *The Impact of the Parent-Child Centers on Parents: A Preliminary Report,* prepared for the Office of Child Development, Contract No. 2997 A/H/O, February 1973, pp. 7–10.

38. Monica B. Holmes, Douglas Holmes, Dorie Greenspan, *The Advocacy Component of Seven Parent-Child Centers: A Final Report on the Start up Year,* prepared for the Office of Child Development, Contract No. 2997 A/H/O, July 1973, p. xvi.

39. U.S. Department of Health, Education, and Welfare, Office of Child Development, "The Home Start Program: Guidelines," December 1971, p. 5.

40. U.S. Department of Health, Education, and Welfare, Office of Child Development, "Home Start Fact Sheet," November 1972; and Ruth Ann O'Keefe, "Home Start: Partnership with Parents," *Children Today,* January-February 1973, pp. 12–15.

41. U.S. Department of Health, Education, and Welfare, Office of Child Development, *The Home Start Demonstration Program: An Overview,* February 1973, pp. 6–8.

42. John F. Hughes and Anne O. Hughes, *Equal Education: A New National Strategy* (Bloomington, Ind.: Indiana University Press, 1972), p. 36.

43. U.S. Congress, House, Hearings Before a Subcommittee of the Committee on Appropriations, *Department of Labor and Health, Education, and Welfare Appropriations for 1974*, Part 2 (Washington: Government Printing Office, 1973), pp. 385–386.

44. *Ibid.*, p. 38.

45. James S. Coleman *et al., Equality of Educational Opportunity* (Washington: Government Printing Office, 1966), p. 229.

LIST OF FIGURES

LIST OF TABLES

INDEX

THE JOHNS HOPKINS UNIVERSITY PRESS

This book was composed in Photon Times Roman type
by Maryland Composition Company from a design by Susan Bishop.
It was printed on 50-lb. International Bookmark paper
and bound in Columbia Atlantic cloth
by Thomson-Shore, Inc.

Library of Congress Cataloging in Publication Data

Levitan, Sar A
  Child care & ABC'S too.

    1. Day care centers—United States. 2. Children of working mothers. 3. Education, Preschool—United States. I. Alderman, Karen Cleary, joint author. II. Title.

HV854.L49   362.7′1   75-11355
ISBN 0-8018-1733-1